The Anasazi of Chaco Canyon:

Greatest Mystery of the
American Southwest

ISBN-13: 978-0692740026

ISBN-10: 0692740023

Shadowplay Communications, LLC
861 Da Vinci Cove
Boulder City, Nevada, USA 89005

First Edition: June 2016

The Anasazi of Chaco Canyon:

Greatest Mystery of the
American Southwest

By Kyle Widner

Dedication

This book is dedicated to the two Angels in my life, for whom I have eternal gratitude:

> Jean Jean, you are the very wind beneath my wings. Without you, I would be forever grounded. I love you with all my heart.

> Mom, you taught me many things, including respect for mother earth. You also tried to teach me to stop and smell the flowers. But turns out I'm allergic to most of them. Is stopping to smell the Juniper okay?

Acknowledgements

Francine Johnson. This book would not have happened without her research, creativity, and wordsmithing.

Howard Analla. Dear friend, warm spirit, and gentle soul. I have very much enjoyed our conversations.

Jill McKellan. A wonderful editor, gentle but firm with this first time author.

Joel Klandrud. Who almost convinced me Chaco was the result of alien technology. And also for the photos that you see throughout this book.

To the whole crew at Milo's, who keeps my glass full and my belly sated, love you all.

To Jean and Mom. Thanks for putting up with me during this whole journey. I promise we can talk about something else now.

Table of Contents

Introduction

Photo of author Kyle Widner standing atop a cave top, searching for Ancient sites in Utah. Most Anasazi ruins are found in south facing caves or alcoves.

This book is about Chaco Canyon, a barren, windswept area of blowing sand located in remote northwestern New Mexico. Words and images alone are not enough to adequately convey the mystery and wonder of this unique place and time in history. This book is broken into three parts. First, the meandering path by which I came to know of, which helped to guide me to my fascination of Chaco Canyon. In the second part, we'll discuss what we know to be true about the phenomenon of Chaco Canyon in the years loosely bounded by 800-1150 AD. Finally, you'll find my interpretation of what occurred; one possible, sweeping scenario of one of the most fascinating chapters in the historical record of North America.

1

The story of how this book came about originates on a unique spit of southwestern geography called Cedar Mesa, in southeast Utah.

Kyle Widner

Part One: Drawn to Chaco Canyon

Kyle Widner

The Raven

For reasons still baffling to me and probably more so to my wife, my draw to Chaco Canyon began years ago, having awoke from a strange dream. It was one of those vivid, realistic dreams that can be confused with reality, until you recognize that it had been a dream, nothing more. Little did I know the journey it would inspire.

While looking down from several thousand feet above, a black bird was flying in perfect circles over what looked to be a non-descript sandstone canyon. With each circle, the spiraling pattern tightened and the bird went lower, corkscrewing toward the canyon floor. There was a sensation of falling, but not like that where you sense you are plunging to a certain death on the jagged rocks below. It was a gentle descent, guided by this graceful black bird as it made its way to the canyon floor. Then the bird's descent ended and I awoke.

My eyes now open, with the dream fresh in my mind, I was more confused than anything else. *Quite random*, I thought. At first, I just ignored it, intrigued, but not overly inspired. But as that day wore on, the vivid imagery stayed alive in my imagination. Over the course of a week or so, my intrigue morphed into a desire to do something that seemed incredibly spontaneous at the time. But first, some background on how I think this came to be.

In 1986 / 1987 my college roommate, Pete Bird, used to tell stories of growing up in Blanding, Utah, a place most people never go to on purpose. He told stories of hunting when he was young, seeing mountain lion tracks that had followed him and his friends, and anecdotal tales of finding Anasazi pottery and artifacts literally strewn around the ground. At the time, I had no frame of reference of the Anasazi, other than a high school 16mm movie on the Hopi of Arizona, a tribe that claims to be descendants of the Anasazi. In the social studies film, the Hopi explain how they do not scold or spank their children, but admonish them softly, saying, "It is not the Hopi way."

With recollections of Pete's stories, I took to Google, devoting a few days to learning about the history and demise of this mysterious group of Native Americans called the Anasazi, and their range in the southwest USA. Then, a few days later, a couple of books on the subject arrived from Amazon. I quickly devoured both and was hooked. It turns out what we were taught in high school American History wasn't quite 100% correct.

Who were the Anasazi?

First, let me get something out of the way. The word Anasazi is attributed to the Navajo language, as a loose translation of "ancient enemy". The Hopi, who also claim to be descendants of the Anasazi, call these ancestors "Hisatsinom", which translates to "Ancient Ones". Over the last 110 years, the name Anasazi has become the generic term for the early Pueblo sites and peoples.

While the Hopi prefer calling these ancestors Hisatsinom, that name is not shared by the Acoma, Zuni, and other Pueblo people who also claim to be descendants from the Ancient Ones. Since the Anasazi left no evidence of a written record we have no idea what they called themselves. Regardless, in academic and politically correct circles it has become vogue to call these ancient peoples "Ancestral Puebloans", the obvious irony being Puebloan is a Spanish word, imposed by ruthless Spanish conquerors in the 1500s.

I have never heard or read of the term Anasazi being used pejoratively, or as a slur, or in any disrespectful manner. To anyone offended by the term Anasazi, I'll invoke my inner Edward Abbey and simply say, "No comment."

To avoid confusion, and for the purpose of familiarity and brevity, in this non-scientific and non-academic book, the term Anasazi refers to the group of Native Americans who occupied the Colorado Plateau up until the abandonment in about 1300 AD. For 1300 and beyond, I'll use the term Puebloan.

After my dream-fueled research binge, I decided to go in search of Anasazi ruins—preferably ruins that were not in the guidebooks. I knew this would be a solo journey, as I don't have any friends or relatives insane enough to go wandering into remote canyons, living like a homeless person for a week. There is one exception, my childhood friend Pat Gish, inconveniently residing in Alabama.

I made some phone calls, sent some emails, and through a series of serendipitous introductions and connections, I found myself invited to spend some time on a large swath of private land where Anasazi ruins were known to be. Careful what you wish for. Now it was time to really prepare myself for the adventure that awaited me.

After a summer of many trips to REI, training locally on remote trails with various footwear and combinations of gear, and evenings spent devouring related books, I was ready. I set off on the 7 hour drive to Cedar Mesa on a warm day in early September.

In my car, I listened to an audio book by author Gary McCarthy called *Mesa Verde*. An entertaining historical fiction tale with a storyline of the "Sun Clan" of New Mexico, and their relationship with the "Raven Clan" of the Mesa Verde area. And just as the book concluded, I pulled into the parking lot of my motel in the sleepy Utah town of Blanding. Once checked in, the not-perky desk clerk robotically handed me a flyer announcing the opening of an Italian restaurant next door to the motel. *Perfect*, I thought. I'll have some pasta, a nice glass of wine, get some sleep, and be ready for the adventure tomorrow. Well, not so much. Think Spaghetti-O's. Actually, I would have preferred a can of Spaghetti-O's. "Excuse me, can I see the wine list?" A quizzical look came across the young server's face, who promptly slid into the booth across from me and said with a dejected look, "Blanding is a dry town. Drives me crazy". Oh.

Kyle Widner

The next morning, meeting over eggs, bacon, and black coffee at the only place in town where breakfast was available, the owner of the land sized me up, probably trying to decide if he was dealing with someone who was a bit crazy or living out some mid-life crisis. Or perhaps, he thought he was dealing with someone who was just plain soft in the skull. I didn't know what he thought and truthfully, it didn't matter. Get me out there; turn me loose, lets rock and roll.

Once he seemed satisfied that he wasn't entering into a situation where there might be a sudden 911 call from a frantic wife or mother looking for their missing wanderer, or guiding a Search and Rescue Operation, we set out. The road was not for the faint of heart, but my newish SUV accepted the beating it was being given and followed his high clearance 4WD pickup truck, a vehicle much better suited to the job. At one point, at a hairpin turn in the rough road, a sweeping view of a meadow at the head of the canyon came into view. An impressive sight. My guide stopped, and as we gazed across the landscape, he began pointing out areas where I'd likely come across Anasazi ruins, cave dwellings, or the remains of pit-houses. Trying to absorb as much of the information as possible, and looking for landmarks to guide me, a trance-like sensation slipped over me. I snapped out of it when he said, "Welcome to Anasazi-ville."

The lands I gazed upon were brilliant with red sandstone formations, bleached white rock, and blanketed with the green of pinyon and juniper, tinged with the gunmetal gray of sage. This land is rarely visited, unknown

Kyle Widner

to the average traveler, not accessible by any public roads or trails. But I had access thanks to a host who asked me to agree upon two conditions: 1) Not dig anything up; and, 2) Not publish the location, or the location of anything discovered. I quickly nodded in agreement, staring at this remarkable, sun-soaked landscape, capped by a sky so blue and bright even the lizards have to squint.

As we came to the bottom of the long, hair-pinned, rocky road, and edged into the meadow previously viewed from above, a sense of isolation began to creep over me. Reading books about the area, pouring over maps, and studying Google Earth was one thing. It was quite another to watch his truck turn around and go back to civilization. (Cue jokes about Blanding and civilization.)

Be careful what you wish for. As the awe of my surroundings faded to reality, a serene quiet settled as the rumbling of his truck faded. I was alone.

I'm not sure if cell phones can laugh, but if they could, I experienced it as I looked down at my iPhone screen, which was giving me a blank, empty look. No service. Might as well turn it off and store it, as it was not going be of any use out here.

While settling in and organizing my gear, the tidbits of advice and information my host offered played repeatedly in my brain like an answering machine tape. The location of a rattlesnake den to watch out for. "Halfway Hill", where hundreds of full and partial arrowheads had been found over the years. Barely visible caves and side canyons with ancient cave dwellings. Locations of springs. I began to orient myself and tried to decide which direction to explore first.

Absorbing it all, I took note of how virgin, pristine the land felt. The air perfumed with juniper. The call of unfamiliar birds. And before me, a canyon complex whispering the remote, but tantalizing possibility of the Holy Grail: an undiscovered and undisturbed cave dwelling, cliff house, or pit-house, stuffed with ancient pottery, tools, and ritual items.

In the land of no guidebooks, the GPS confirmed my location on the map. I organized my gear, checked the time, made my plan, and took off for an afternoon hike.

I followed along a shallow wash running along a northern sandstone cliff, and the first promised site came into view. A cave, possibly occupied as far back as the Basketmaker Era, more than 1,500 years ago. Exactly where the owner said it would be.

Looking at this cave I was amazed at what I saw through appreciative eyes, the past emerging and unfolding before me. Pottery sherds, corncobs, chert, and broken arrowheads strewn across the mouth of the cave, along with a thousand plus years of soot baked into the top of the naturally formed shelter.

Kyle Widner

Basketmaker era cave; showing centuries of soot from cooking and warming that have built up on the top of this cave, which could date back 1,500 years.

All by myself, exploring history and Anasazi life from long ago. It was the first of many incredible moments, and everything I hoped it would be.

But it was time to move on…

As I made my way to the next location, I stopped by a spring to refill my water. Soon after, heading down a game trail through shoulder high grass, a crashing sound rudely startled me, something unexpected, unwelcomed. It was the sound of a very large animal moving quickly behind some brush just up ahead. Startled, I instinctively froze. What was it? A bear, elk, mountain lion? Moving slowly and watchfully, and making a comically wide detour, I eased down the trail.

After a bit of distance, constantly looking back, I identified the source of the racket. Ahhh! The adversary appeared—a freaking cow. Who had startled whom? After a good chuckle, I imagined the eye roll of my country girl mother. There I was, my first day on Cedar Mesa, and a freaking cow sent me scurrying. I named her Betsie, bowed slightly, apologized for any trouble, and headed down the trail to the next cave site.

The trail wound up into a boxed-in canyon, through some magnificent terrain. The rich, red soil, brilliant blue sky, and green of the trees merged into a dreamy landscape, incredibly peaceful. The only man-made intrusions were the occasional jets flying overhead, bringing travelers of the day between Denver and the cities further southwest. Those cities were far away now, as if a foreign land.

At the head of this box canyon was a huge fold inside a sandstone cliff, perhaps a quarter mile across. It was not a deep enough recess to be called a cave, but the overhanging cliff, some 250' above, would have provided shelter from most rain and snow, but equally as important, shade from the relentless summer afternoon sun. Almost all cliff and cave dwellings open facing south, to capture as much winter sun as possible. One ruin on Cedar Mesa provides an exception to this south-only rule, earning it the name "Wrong Way Ruin". The ruins I was now standing before contained perhaps 15 pueblo structures. Pictographs and petroglyphs, corncobs, charcoal, and pottery sherds strewn everywhere, and the tell tale signs of grave robbers, also known as "pot hunters", their holes dug and not refilled, with the piles of earth next to the scars of their test pits.

800+ year old corncobs, charred but intact, and an unidentified animal tooth found at this site.

Pot Hunters

On June 10th, 2009, a tactical assault force of heavily armed FBI agents swarmed the heavily Mormon town of Blanding, Utah, population 3600. Waving automatic weapons, the FBI shackled 17 local citizens at the wrists, ankles, and waist. Their ages ranged from 27 to 73. Among these was the respected town physician, Dr. James Redd, age 60, a member of the Utah Tourism Hall of Fame, as well as the county sheriff's brother, a high school teacher. They were faced with more than 100 felony counts of stealing Indian and government property, and illegally buying and selling artifacts. Obviously, the handling of ancient artifacts is serious business.

In the Blanding part of the world, digging for and collecting artifacts predates the founding of Blanding in 1905. Homes in this sparsely populated area uniformly feature pots, arrowheads, and other artifacts that adorn shelves and mantles. Many are found on private land, where digging and collecting remains legal; however, proving provenance is difficult, if not impossible, especially if not documented at the time of collection. Those who pursue the illegal collection of these artifacts on public lands are engaging in illegal "pot hunting" and are responsible for the destruction of many delicate Anasazi ruins and archaeological sites. I have personally witnessed the aftermath of this type of destruction at the Turkey Pen ruin site in Grand Gulch.

Sadly, Dr. James Redd, father of five, so traumatized by the FBI raid and the stain on his reputation,

15

committed suicide the day after his arrest by connecting a hose to the exhaust pipe of his car. In a wrongful death suit filed by his widow, it stated Dr. Redd was arrested for a felony, and "manhandled" for hours in his garage. The "physical and psychological assault" on him focused on his family, religion, profession, and community. The specific felony charge? Possession of a single effigy bird pendant, found on a family walk.

That day, as I looked at the broken pottery, corncobs, charcoal, and other remnants of Anasazi life scattered before me, Dr. Redd's story played over in my head. If he would have found that same object here, on private land, he might still be alive today. It's a conflict I wrestle with. I have utter disdain for illegal pot hunters that disturb or ruin ancient sites for greedy, selfish reasons. However, I feel equal disgust that our own federal government would take such extreme action and traumatize a respected small-town doctor to the point he found suicide to be the solution.

Pondering the Pursuit

Letting the Dr. Redd story go, I relaxed and reflected in the solitude of this magnificent place, my eyes closed, and my mind drifted off to some form of deep rest. I was jolted back to the present by the sound of small rocks tumbling down the cliff face. The sun was getting low so I gathered myself, and avoiding the area of the rattlesnake den, made my way back to base camp, hungry for supper and eager for reflection.

That evening, Cedar Mesa opened the treasure box, delivering a spectacular sunset, blazing near the horizon, slowly muting the colors of the landscape before sensuously retiring behind the red sandstone cliffs. As the sun left for the day, I munched on hot dogs and canned chili, washed down with generous rations of my favorite cheap travel wine, YellowTail Shiraz / Cabernet blend, packaged conveniently in 1.5 liter bottles with a screw top. Bigger bottles = less overall packaging material.

Sitting with smug satisfaction at my environmental friendliness, serious star watching was now in order. Unbeknownst to me ahead of time, this was to be a moonless night, and the display of stars, shooting and static, was incredible. It was hard not to see a shooting star at any one time, and the clear, predictable path of a manmade satellite was visible as it streaked across the dark sky. It was then that I realized I had never seen the full beauty of the Milky Way in real life, only in pictures. Also, I'd never seen stars so close to the horizon before. I chuckled internally at my city-boy-ness.

Kyle Widner

Once I'd had my fill, and dreading the heartburn that sometimes follows one too many hot dogs, I popped a handful of Tums as a preventative measure, and stored the balance of my wine safely in the ice chest with the broken latch. Ice is civilization, and therefore, I decided to place my boots on top of the cooler to maintain the seal. Time to fall asleep. Well, try to fall asleep. The silence was so, well, silent. I awoke several times during a night so quiet it almost seemed sterile. Every gentle breeze rustling the brush or trees, every twitch of a rabbit, deer, or mouse was amplified and put me on alert. I could hear the field mice scurrying about their business. Coyotes sang their songs and chased their prey; I imagined a terrified rabbit about to be reduced to a puff of white fur that I'd see along the trail the next day.

Kyle Widner

A New Day

I awoke to a spectacular morning, pissed in the open like free men do, walked around, and then contemplated and prioritized the morning needs. Coffee! Waiting for water to boil, deep breaths rose and fell naturally, filling my lungs with fresh, fragrant air. Coffee was sipped, and dehydrated oatmeal proved to be a satisfying meal to start the day. Deciding to take a long day hike and reconnoiter down-canyon, I stuffed the daypack with the essentials; map, compass, GPS, jerky, cashews, Kind bars, camera, and first aid kit. The bladder of the CamelBak was filled, shoelaces retied tightly, Gaiters secured, pack swung on and adjusted for snugness. Sunscreen applied, Chapstick daubed, wide hat, polarized sunglasses, and keffiyeh loosely wrapped around my neck. GPS powered on, waypoint marked, and a final look around to orient with the visible landmarks. Feeling quite expeditious, I headed down-canyon, navigating a remote, though not difficult passage dotted with juniper, pinyon, sage, prickly pear cacti, and various grasses intermingled between the sandstone.

The soil is red, the sky is blue and the junipers are green, and a sense of adventure settles within me, a feeling long dormant, eroded away by the persistent responsibilities of adult life.

Discoveries from the day before had been so easy, leaving me to expect that I'd have the same fortune as I explored the day's sandstone niches and side canyons—all the while keeping an alert eye downward for snakes and upward for ruins. Again, I saw cattle meandering about and found water, fresh from a spring, but it required filtering to eliminate the chance of "Beaver Fever". This is a well known process, mandatory for anyone who wants to drink from a water source in cattle country. Until now, it hadn't even occurred to me that so much of Cedar Mesa was open range. The cattle were common there; I, the city-boy explorer was the invader, the interloper, the spoiler.

Near midday, I stopped on a sandstone ledge and enjoyed a leisurely lunch of cashews and beef jerky, which when combined, makes a very satisfying and tasty gruel in the mouth. A positive side effect of this snack is making you thirsty and wanting to drink more water. This is very important, as dehydration is a real threat in canyon country. Not only because of the high temperatures and direct heat from the sun, but at 6200' above sea level, and combined with the arid climate, dehydration can come quickly. Realizing I hadn't watered any cactus since early morning, I decided to drink water until nature called.

Upon resuming my exploration, I spied a side canyon that stirred my imagination. I could see southern facing indentions in the sandstone, but without field glasses, couldn't be sure if there was anything interesting to see up there. However, it seemed to have all the elements you look for when searching for Anasazi sites, including some dense green patches that could indicate a water source. My imagination raced with the possibilities. Assessing the ascent, it looked like no more than a tricky scramble up a talus slope to get to a ledge I could walk along.

Your author.

Let me say here, I am deathly afraid of heights. I literally get vertigo, and my feet don't work right. This particular climb pushed me to my maximum comfortable limit, but I decided to keep going a bit farther, thinking that as I followed the ledge further up-canyon, it would somehow, magically get wider and easier to follow, opening up into an undiscovered Mesa Verde style cliff dwelling. In my mind, I'd jumped to the future and was practicing my award acceptance speech at the next conference of Southwest Archaeologists. Instead, I came to a realization—I was now stuck on a ledge that simply disappeared into a nearly vertical crumble of sandstone debris, and at a point so narrow that there was no turning around, literally.

Looking down, I sized up the results of a potential fall. The fall, in and of its self, wouldn't be fatal, just bone-snappingly painful. However, knowing I was somewhere I'd probably never be found if something bad happened did not improve my mood.

My only choice was to slowly and carefully start moving backwards, which I did with great patience, a trait for which I am not well known.

Once the ledge was wide enough for me to kneel down and reach an outcropping below, I was able to maneuver down, rock by rock, and eventually reached the mouth of the side canyon and back to the main canyon. With a deep sigh, I sat down and mentally declared that I'd used up my quota of stupid for the trip.

But little did I know, I had a reserve of non-so-bright left in me…

As the high sun began to tilt toward mid-afternoon I felt a twinge of disappointment. I hadn't found any ruins or pit-house sites, not even a flipping sherd of pottery or broken arrowhead. I looked at my GPS and began to head back up-canyon, stopping at the same spring to filter more water, which I was drinking at a rapid rate. Refreshed, I had a brief conversation with a confused cow blocking my path, a one-way conversation, as I don't think she quite understood what I was asking. Once cleared of her, I picked up my pace toward the car, now eagerly anticipating a cold, refreshing adult beverage from the cooler. Mexican Gatorade: Corona beer, lotsa lime, lotsa salt. Yum.

As I walked along the spine between two fingers of the canyon, weaving between pinyons, sage, and rocks slicking out of the earth like broken teeth, I wasn't fully paying attention, feeling somewhat fatigued from wandering around all day in the desert sun. At an opening in the trees, I came across an arrangement of stones that looked a bit out of place, rocks in a circular pattern. Scanning the scene, my eyes began spotting pieces of pottery and some broken arrowheads nearby. I looked closer and realized the rocks were the remains of a circular foundation, perhaps a pit-house or storage room. Discovery!

Dropping my pack and scurrying around on my hands and knees, all the classic remains of a pit-house site were present, and as a bonus, there was a somewhat rare stone-digging tool. Everything you'd expect to find, except for… Wait, a rusted tin can? Well, obviously I wasn't the first one to find the site, but it did not temper my excitement. The pottery was almost exclusively Mancos Black on White and corrugated greyware, dating the site to about 1150-1250 AD.

This was it, and I was incredibly excited. I made sketches and took photographs, remembering my pledge not to dig. The temptation did cross my mind, but I was in the land of the Spiritwalker, and needed to remember my role. Sadly, the sun was really beginning to sink into the horizon, spurring my departure, which was tough. I grabbed my pack, took several last photographs, and headed back toward the car, my mind now abuzz with what I'd just seen, my pace quickened by the adrenalin.

Taking a quick stop to pull an energy bar from the pack, I checked the GPS. Not too bad—only about a half mile as the crow flies to the car. Confident of my exact location, I stuffed the GPS in the pack, commencing to march dutifully on.

Several minutes later, expecting to be near the car, I was startled to come face-to-face with a small, but deep and impassible canyon directly between me and where my car would be. Momentarily dazed and confused, I found the source of my error on my map. I had simply come up the wrong ridge; I needed to be on the ridge to the west of me. Checking my track on the GPS, ah, no problem, I just needed to head back down and find out where I had crossed that morning. Again, I stowed the GPS, confident it would be obvious when I reached the crossing point.

Only it wasn't. Dense brush and tangles of trees made passage slow. Beginning to feel confused, I re-checked the GPS and found I had passed where the track said I had come across that morning, and disturbingly, the travel line on the GPS was arrow straight. I'd gone up and down so many washes, gullies, and arroyos that day but didn't remember this one, especially not a straight route. Making my way back to where I'm supposed to be according to the GPS, I still can't see it. Thick brush and large rocks confused the scene. My mind was seized by the beginnings of panic when I looked again at the straight line on the GPS. Had I lost signal or power that morning and it was simply connecting points? Could the GPS be wrong? Military training flashed back into my mind from 20 years earlier, telling me, *calm down, evaluate, make a plan, and execute the plan.*

Drawing a deep breath, I sat on a rock and gnawed on a piece of beef jerky, not wanting my irritability at the situation to influence my decision-making. Deciding on a solution, I would continue going down-canyon until I could find a place to cross. Not ideal, but annoying.

As I reached for my pack to get moving, not wanting to get stuck in the dark, a lone cloud passed in front of the late afternoon sun, and the shadow caused me to look up. While looking up at the blocked sun, a raven sat on top of a pinyon, looking directly at me while lecturing me with his echoing croak. I smiled as I recalled the audio book from the day before, talking about the Sun Clan and the Raven Clan, not to mention my dream that had started this entire experience. Was the bird in the dream a raven? There was the sun, hidden behind a cloud, and the raven scolding me. Suddenly, the raven flew off across the canyon. With a chuckle, I thought to myself, *wouldn't it make a cool story if the raven were showing me the way across the canyon?* As I worked my way through the tight brush and rocks toward where the raven had been sitting, I was startled to see my boot prints from that morning in the soft red clay. Punching through one more tangle, I saw the path I had used, clear as day. I was where I needed to be.

25

I whisked across to the other side of the canyon, and with tired legs trudging the last few steps to my car, I sucked the last slurp of water from my CamelBak. In the process, I made a promise to myself to never tell the story, less I sound like a crazy person who'd spent too much time in the sun.

Fortunately, that was my only drama of my first trip to Cedar Mesa, and the rest of the week was filled with long hikes, stiff muscles, and sandstone solitude. Evenings were pleasantly predictable, highlighted by peaceful star watching aside a small fire. A concluding highlight was a night spent in Grand Gulch, beneath Junction Ruins, a cliff dwelling so high on the cliff wall, I could see no possible way of reaching it by climbing. However, they carried building supplies, food, water, and firewood up there. Color me impressed.

Since then, I've been back to Cedar Mesa many times, with countless day hikes and overnight excursions in this enchanting landscape of stone, earth, and sun.

Dwelling on the Past in a Civilized World

Eventually, I did relay my raven story to a good friend, Howard Analla, who is a member of the Laguna Pueblo tribe in New Mexico. Expecting a dismissive eye roll from Howard, he instead said, without hesitation, "The raven is your totem. You don't choose your totem, your totem chooses you." Then he shared his own raven story with me, a story so beautifully haunting that it brought tears to my eyes. Over time, and through many subsequent conversations, Howard also helped me to realize that there is magic in simply paying attention to the world around you, and oftentimes, this is mistaken for shamanic or spiritual power.

Part Two: Chaco Canyon and the Anasazi

Chaco Brought to Light

No one can study the history of the southwest USA, or the peoples of the prehistoric North America continent without coming across the fascinating tale of the Anasazi. And any story of the Anasazi will reference Mesa Verde National Park, located near the quaint, old-west-meets-hipster town of Cortez in the southwest corner of Colorado. Most people end up visiting the cliff dwelling ruins of "Cliff Palace" at Mesa Verde, and come away believing these structures represent the pinnacle of the Anasazi culture, the Upper East Side of Manhattan, if you will, of Anasazi existence. Many absorb in the spectacle that is Mesa Verde, and think of it as the "grand finale", as this is where the Anasazi peaked and "disappeared" from. I know I did, at the time. But like they say in infomercials, "But wait, there's more!"

Mesa Verde is Spanish for "green table". As the park rangers love to point out, Mesa Verde is actually a "cuesta", not a mesa. Mesas are flat on top, and cuestas drain off to one side. In the case of Mesa Verde, the entire drainage flows south, into the Mancos River, then into the San Juan, to the Colorado River, winds through the Grand Canyon, and finally to the Pacific Ocean.

Cliff Palace, Spruce Tree House, Sun Temple, and countless other ruins and archaeological sites at Mesa Verde speak to the advanced cultural, agricultural, and architectural achievements of the Anasazi during their time there. 550,000 visitors annually visit Mesa Verde, and the

Kyle Widner

vast majority come away awed by what they have seen. But what is the connection to Chaco?

In a broad, generalized review, the Anasazi timeline of the area is something like this:

- The Anasazi were well entrenched in and around Mesa Verde for centuries. In the early to mid 800s AD, unstable climate and unpredictable rains foreshadowed a migration from the Mesa Verde area south to the San Juan Basin, which includes Chaco Canyon.
- By 950, Chaco Canyon had replaced Mesa Verde as the nexus of the Anasazi world, and it remained that way for almost 200 years.
- By 1150, for reasons that can only be speculated upon, not proven, the reverse occurred, and the Anasazi began migrating back to Mesa Verde. This is when the cliff dwellings of Mesa Verde were constructed.

The most famous of these dwellings is Cliff Palace, built and remodeled between the years 1190-1260, according to tree-ring dating. As we'll see, the architecture and engineering of Mesa Verde, while impressive, is but residue and afterthought compared to the more spectacular achievements of the Anasazi in Chaco Canyon.

Why is Mesa Verde so well known and visited while Chaco Canyon is not? Several factors are at play. Mesa Verde is located in a beautifully forested, scenic area with crisp, long range views of snowcapped peaks, easily accessible by paved roads, in a park with a first class lodge, restaurant and bar, a deluxe campground with showers, and a well-stocked camp store. Visitors have access to regularly scheduled ranger-guided tours, with tickets purchased in advance. The park is an easy drive from Cortez, Colorado.

As the raven flies, Chaco Canyon is about 85 miles south / southeast from Mesa Verde, with Farmington, New Mexico smack dab in the middle of the imaginary line between the two locations.

Chaco Canyon flourished in the Anasazi world with achievements that dwarf Mesa Verde, yet it receives only about 50,000 visitors per year, less than 10% of Mesa Verde National Park. Chaco's fluorescence and decline occurred prior to the construction of the cliff dwellings of Mesa Verde. Chaco, whose ruins are nowhere near as well restored as the cliff dwellings of Mesa Verde, is considered a stepchild, if visitor counts are considered.

None of the modern amenities exist in Chaco Canyon. The closest lodging is an hour and a half drive on mostly dirt roads, when in good condition. To come in from the east, the traveler is faced with an equally daunting trek; portions of the unpaved roads are easily washed out by summer thunderstorms, leaving bone jarring ruts. Once you make it to the park you are greeted with only a limited, basic campground, offering zero shade in summer and no respite from the deviously cold winds that roll in later in the year. And if you're lucky enough to be at Chaco in the spring, prepare to be blasted by pervasive and abrasive sand in impressive quantities, traveling at equally impressive velocity.

A secondary factor I've noticed first hand is that the ruins of Mesa Verde simply "make sense". The defensive nature of the architecture is easy to understand and it takes little imagination to visualize people at work and play, secure and protected from incursion. The restored ruins are clearly identifiable as housing, storage granaries, and watch towers. The access points are difficult to move through and around, obviously a measure designed for defense. Green, well-watered agricultural areas abound upon the mesa. Rangers talk, tourists gawk and nod.

Chaco, on the other hand leaves most people impressed, but very confused. Furling of the brow. Quizzical expressions. Almost nothing makes sense. Rough, barren terrain. No obvious water sources. No natural resources. Massive buildings with scant evidence of habitation. Only a small portion of the ruins restored, much left to the imagination.

When you compare Mesa Verde's museum-quality, manicured, ranger-guided, air conditioned, tour bus style visitation with Chaco Canyon's desolate "you're on your own" experience, one can see why Mesa Verde receives eleven times more visitors annually than Chaco.

Chaco inspires its own sense of wonder and awe, but deeply blended with a healthy dose of blank-stare confusion.

Kyle Widner

The location of Chaco makes zero sense to modern sensibilities—a wide, shallow, windswept dirt wash, not located near any known resources. The Great Houses of Chaco are truly magnificent, and almost comically impressive, but the archaeological record reveals few actual residents. Why build a 700 room building that is 4 stories high; larger than anything before or since, and not populate it? Then, while you are chewing on that, why build several more, also never occupied by more than a several dozen people? The buildings in Chaco required a total of approximately 240,000 logs, each about 60' long. These were cut down and hand-hauled across rough, unforgiving terrain from over 50 miles away, a feat even more impressive when you consider the Anasazi Chacoans did not have the wheel or draft animals. This astounding outcome was 100% human powered. The logistics and sheer calories or energy expended staggers the imagination. And, just for fun, incalculable tons of sandstone had to be sourced, mined, shaped, and mortared together to create the masonry of the Great Houses, and all without metal tools.

The feeling of Chaco is one of complete isolation from the outside world. There is no distant horizon visible from within the canyon. One feels "wrapped" inside a blanket of sandstone.

Okay, so who were these enigmatic people that simply "vanished" in 1300? We're all familiar with the story of the populating of the Americas when early migrations crossed the Bering Sea and began pushing through the North American continent. About 6500-1200 BC, in the Four Corners region of the southwest USA, a distinct culture began to form, pre-Anasazi, if you will. This is called the Archaic Period, and they lived a peaceful existence, with limited competition for resources. They depended on primitive farming and supplemented their diet with wild berries, nuts, and hunting. Shelter was provided by natural caves, and according to archaeologists, these pre-Anasazi peoples faced few enemies.

About 1200 BC, they began to weave baskets from willow and other fibrous plant materials. By spreading pinyon gum on the inside of these baskets, they could be made waterproof. This marks the beginning of the early Basketmaker Era, also known as Basketmaker I. They were not yet making clay or ceramic pottery.

In approximately 50 AD, there is evidence of more permanent dwellings being constructed, including shallow pit-houses and storage bins, kicking off the Basketmaker II Era.

About 500 AD, pit-houses became deeper, up to 5' below ground, supplemented by some purely above ground structures, including dedicated storage rooms. The bow and arrow appeared, replacing the spear and the dart-throwing atlatl as the primary hunting tool. Some plain pottery began appearing. This Basketmaker III Era ended in 750 AD, and crude masonry dwellings began replacing pit-houses. Pottery went from being purely plain and utilitarian to showing some painted designs, kicking off the Pueblo I Period.

Pueblo I (750-900 AD) saw pit-houses fading away, and replaced by more elaborate above ground masonry structures. Pueblo II (900-1150) is the period sections two and three of this book will address in more detail. Ceremonial chambers called kivas began to appear, likely evolving from nostalgia or connection to now seldom-used pit-houses. Construction ranged from simple to unbelievably incredible. Ornate pottery, jewelry making, and large trading networks flourished.

Pueblo III (1150-1350) is the sad chapter in the history of these fascinating ancient people. Forced into living in high cliff walls as a defensive measure, squeezed by drought, disease, starvation, and the appearance of ruthless raiding parties from the north, a great civilization collapsed. Their population decimated, they dispersed to pueblos along the Rio Grande until the 1500s when the Spanish arrived, greedy for gold, and the 1700s, when westward expansion of the young United States was not to be stopped.

In high school, the story was the Anasazi simply faded into the ether, leaving dinner on plates and just up and vanishing into thin air. Great story for a Twilight Zone episode, but not true. In reality, there was a massive depopulation and migration about the year 1300, when they dispersed. The descendants of the Anasazi live with us today in the 19 Pueblo tribes along the Rio Grande River, which flows through Albuquerque, NM, as well as the Zuni and Hopi tribes. Part Three of this book is a historically based, but fictional, narrative of one possible scenario of this period.

Kyle Widner

This Part Two, which you are currently reading, explores what we know about Chaco Canyon from the archaeological and anthropological records the Chacoans left behind. This is not meant to be an exhaustive review of the existing research, but an overview of what we know, and to an even greater degree, what we don't know. Any errors, omissions, misrepresentations, or other silliness is the sole responsibility of your author.

Environment of Chaco Canyon

Chaco Canyon. Barren and desolate, leaving visitors asking, "Why here?"

The San Juan River Basin is a massive, 150 mile oval depression that originates in Colorado, and snakes through New Mexico and Utah on its way to the mighty Colorado River, through the Grand Canyon, and finally to the Pacific Ocean.

Within this mighty basin we find thousands of archaeological sites reflecting the ancient civilization known as the Anasazi. Chaco is a remote tributary of the San Juan, a desolate 20-mile section best described as a sandy wash, draining north into the San Juan River.

The southwest USA is usually thought of as a hot, dry climate, when in fact it is amazingly diverse in geology and geography. Chaco Canyon has an unforgiving climate, with bone chilling winters featuring sharp, biting winds, and roasting summers that can send the hardiest souls

37

scurrying to the cover of shade in the mid-day sun. At 6,200' above sea level, Chaco is colder, longer, than most people would assume. According to the data collected between 1941 and 1970, the canyon averages only 150 frost-free days per year; (Vivian and Mathews 3). Staying warm would have required continual fire, clothing, and shelter.

The Anasazi Indians that occupied this canyon are commonly referred to as "Chacoans". To these resilient residents, there were two overwhelming concerns to their daily existence that would have ultimately meant the difference between life and death; water and warmth. Imagine what it would take to obtain, store, and judiciously use water in an environment such as this; one with less than 9" of annual rainfall.

A reflection of this uninviting terrain was noted during the Hyde Expedition (1896-1901), where S.J. Holsinger wrote this of his Chaco experience:

> *"The only tolerable season is June to October. During this period the rains occur and nature exerts herself to redeem the desert. However, at best the scattering vegetation only lends a blending of green to the somber brown and yellow of the landscape."* (Lister and Lister 50).

The climate and location of Chaco are the first in a series of truly confounding mysteries surrounding the people and environment of this otherwise non-descript location. You cannot visit and explore the canyon without wondering, *why here?* Yet, here they built, and on a massive scale, and lived for over 200 years.

Paleo-environmental studies suggest the vegetation in the canyon has changed little in the past 2,000 years, creating a natural curiosity about agriculture. With the canyon's high elevation, aridity, low seasonal precipitation, and cold winters (short growing season); cultivation had to be a challenge then, just as it would be now. We can only speculate, as agriculture is difficult to track, forensically, organic matter rarely surviving exposure and time.

Chaco Wash, itself, is an ephemeral stream and the major drainage system of the high interior basin, splitting the Chaco plateau in half, dividing it from east to west; (Lister and Lister 180). The presence of water is what you would expect in any desert canyon; ferocious flooding after rains, with lingering, remnant pools, and then bone dry after evaporation in the baking sun.

Climbing up out of the main canyon and scanning the horizon, the mountains where the Chaco River commences can be seen in the Continental Divide, near Star Lake, at an elevation of 6,900'. After meandering westerly through Chaco Canyon and beyond for some 70+ miles, the Chaco takes an abrupt turn northward and merges with the San Juan River. The San Juan Basin drainage consists almost entirely of sandstone and shale, eroded into broad flat surfaces, creating a stark, yet striking environment.

Rain in this part of the world is a fickle beast; rarely coming down as a steady patter over long periods of time. Normally, the skies open up and a deluge crashes down from the heavens in a fury, rushing down side canyons and off the canyon tops, filled with silt and rocks. Controlling this wild runoff would have been necessary to store or redirect it toward soil suitable for agriculture and daily use.

We would expect there to have been at least one perennial water source, but the only source that can be determined as a reliable is a saline pool in Escavada Wash; (Vivian 34).

Additional research by Gordon Vivian and Mathews found annual precipitation averaging 8.7" per year. Yet, there is danger in the term "average" when talking about desert rainfall. 17" of rain in a one year, and a single inch the next would still leave you with an average of 9" per year, but that second year would have been life threatening. The Chacoans never knew what they were going to receive in terms of rainfall, making planning and preparation a life and death proposition.

Evidence of check dams, canals, and irrigation ditches have been found. Logically, this makes sense. The largest volumes of water would come suddenly, and storing it until needed would be crucial. There are three parts of this control system. First would be check dams at the bottom of side canyons and other outlets where the floodwaters would emerge. Second would be irrigation control ditches to divert the water to the fields where crops could use it, while shielding the crops from devastating flooding. Finally, collecting the water in "ollas", which are pottery containers designed specifically for holding (drinking)water until it is needed, likely storing them in residential areas.

Aggraded alluvium soil was held within an area suitable for floodwater control and irrigation. This alluvium within Chaco Canyon is derived from both the headwaters of the drainage and from the Chacra Mesa—the south wall of Chaco Canyon;(Vivian and Mathews).It's also interesting to note that Chacra Mesa was also a possible primary source of daily firewood in Chacoan days, even though it is mostly barren today.

The southern side of the canyon is noticeably more sloped than the northern side, and the presence of multiple small housing units leads to speculation this is where most of the agriculture would have taken place. The southern cliffs would have offered shade during the hot growing months, reducing the evaporation of ground moisture. This would have also made them more ideal locations for agriculture.

Corn, or maize, was the Chacoans main crop, a staple for food and possibly trade. However, some agriculturalists doubt the ability to farm corn, at least good corn, in the saline soil of the canyon. It is speculated that the bulk of the corn was grown in the outlying areas and imported into Chaco Canyon, and the Great Houses were more ceremonial than residential.

Kyle Widner

But, alas, like most all things Chaco, the depth and breadth of agriculture is also a debated topic:

> *"Some archaeologists wholly believe that Chaco was a thriving agricultural society.*
> *"Seeds and other food remains are common at Chacoan settlements. At Pueblo Bonito, squash seeds were found in at least fifty rooms, corncobs, husks, or silks in at least forty-five. Hardly what one would expect of a ceremonial center with allegedly empty rooms..."* (Plog 57).

While there is a consensus that agriculture was a key factor of life in Chaco, it would have been highly unlikely that Chaco could support all that lived there. Furthermore, with the extensive and intensive efforts to construct the Great Houses, a lack of agriculture to feed the workers would have made that an impossible task to accomplish without importing food. During this time of the building of the Great Houses, known as the "Bonito Phase", evidence of a far-flung trade network exists.

> *"The Bonito Phase is famous for evidence of long-distance exchange in materials, especially pottery, turquoise, macaws, cacao, and timber and therefore it is reasonable to think that food could have moved through these same exchange systems."* (Drake et al).

Kyle Widner

These trade routes are an intriguing issue to explore. Logistically, to get supplies to and from Chaco meant having to traverse one of the most barren landscapes in the world. There would have been established trade routes, well-worn paths, and many groups converging on these routes into and out of Chaco proper. A confusing system of "roads" has been discovered, another baffling mystery of Chaco. Many academics do not believe that Chacoans actually used these massive roads for trade, despite their existence leading to that obvious conclusion. Why create the roads then? After all, the surrounding geography must have been daunting for all who made the pilgrimage to Chaco. Since they were capable of building roads, wouldn't it make sense to build them to facilitate trade and travel to and from the canyon proper? These thoughts simply add to fascination, knowing a conclusion is likely never to be reached.

Traveling upon the northern mesas and cliffs, looking for the remnants of these roads, you'll also find grasses, rabbit brush, Mormon tea, and yucca. Moving over to the southern slopes of the Chacra Mesa, there are the familiar ground cover plants, plus juniper and pinyon pine; (Lister and Lister 182).

Some consider Chacra Mesa to have once been woodland, which would have been a convenient wood supply point. However, the large wooden beams used in the construction of the Great Houses have been documented to be from distances of 50-100 miles away, including the San Mateo Mountains. The Chacra Mesa supply was likely used for firewood, tools, and perhaps small construction.

43

Today, what we find in this area is quite different. The modern-day visitor sees a landscape choked with tumbleweeds that have besieged the canyon. This tumbleweed (Salsola Kali) is not an indigenous species, and its invasion has displaced local native grasses, threatening the native four-wing saltbush; (Hanna and Hanna).

Smaller animals in the canyon include the usual desert assortment of cottontail bunnies, mice, and squirrels. There are gophers, kangaroo rats, prairie dogs, bobcats, badgers, and snakes. Overnight stays at the Gallo Campground will find the visitor serenaded with the haunting hoots of owls and distinct cry of the coyote. An elk herd occupies the canyon, though these magnificent animals are seldom seen during the day. On the canyon tops, pronghorn antelope continue to roam as they have for thousands of years.

Gallo Campground: the only "lodging" available in Chaco Canyon. RV hookups and tent pads. Precious little shade in summer, vicious sandstorms in spring, and cold biting winds in winter.

Finally, let's conclude this section with an overview of the primary human feature integrated into Chaco: the phenomenon of the Great House. We'll discover the alignment and position of these monstrous buildings was no accident; it was driven by astronomical alignments and perhaps other ritual factors we have yet to consider. The Great Houses are overwhelmingly built along the northern canyon wall, to best absorb the precious, warming sunlight of the lower winter sun.

The Una Vida and Peñasco Blanco Great Houses are strategically located at both ends of the canyon, with commanding views. Pueblo del Arroyo has a view directly through South Gap. But a strange twist of positioning surrounds Pueblo Bonito. While it has precise alignment to the midday sun, it was also constructed directly beneath a massive chunk of sandstone known as Threatening Rock, perched precariously and partially detached from the canyon wall. The descriptions of some of the earliest written history of archaeology include descriptions of Threatening Rock, before its fall:

> *"An immense rock hung over Pueblo Bonito*
> *and you could see there was a crack behind*
> *it. It had been walled up and timbers put*
> *beneath it to keep it from falling over on the*
> *ruin..."* (Gabriel 47).

Indeed, it eventually fell in 1941, and crushed a large swatch of the back of the ruins of Pueblo Bonito. Today, the park service trail around Pueblo Bonito climbs through this debris field.

The environment of Chaco Canyon is one of harshness and mystery. We'll never know the answer to "why here", but we can experience one connection with the ancient inhabitants. When in Chaco, there is no horizon you can see past, no distance visible of any kind. The canyon itself is your complete world. This creates a strange, but oddly comforting feeling that one can't help but speculate was part of the draw.

Inhabitation and Population

Like most everything Chaco, we're left to imagine what life would have been like for the inhabitants. We know there were small houses, outlying Chacoan communities, and the magnificent Great Houses. Who lived in each, and why? These questions have stumped archaeologists, anthropologists, and visitors alike. It's tempting to believe the rulers or chiefs lived in the Great Houses, the worker bees lived in the small houses, and the farmers lived in the outlier communities.

A highly respected interpreter at Chaco Canyon National Historic Park, G.B. Cornucopia, makes an analogy that to the Chacoans the Great Houses would have been where the kings or chiefs of the community lived, just as we associate the White House in Washington, DC with where our president lives. It's a residential building, but also highly symbolic. Furthermore, acting as a *residence* is not the primary function of the White House, or, seemingly, the Great Houses. Another analogy is the Vatican in Rome. The Vatican is a huge complex stuffed with treasures of immense value, opulent architecture, but sparsely inhabited; there seem to be some parallels with the Chacoan Great Houses.

The Great Houses certainly must have housed some part of the population, but there is no evidence that these were apartment buildings were teeming with citizens, as one would expect of buildings with 700 individual rooms. The Great Houses were clearly meant for a certain class of

Kyle Widner

people, which is inconsistent when compared to Anasazi life before, and the Puebloan cultures that followed.

If Chaco, in its prime, *was* a social structure of extreme hierarchies, it would be unique in the ancient Anasazi world. Evidence of a hierarchal social structure does exist in the ornate burials of Room 33 of Pueblo Bonito Great House. Room 33 is a small, otherwise nondescript room with 13 elaborate, ornate burials unseen anywhere else. Also, burials in Pueblo Bonito indicate that some members of society were, at the very least, better fed than others. These members were taller than the average community member, and exhibited less of the dietary afflictions common at the time. This reiterates the belief that the Great Houses were for those of higher rank within the society, and the community likely supported these persons of upper-class status.

There appears to be additional evidence of hierarchal structure found in the physical layout of the Great Houses, in relation to one and other, and in relation to the small houses. These residences may have been active political homes. The theory of elite residences is supported by archaeology professor, Stephen Lekson. Lekson states in *The Chaco Meridian* that he does not believe that the Great Houses served any purpose other than as elite palaces:

> *"Chaco Canyon was perhaps the most obvious example of 'stratified housing' in archaeology...the major Great Houses were so very markedly different from normal houses, the ubiquitous unit pueblo...Great*

Houses and unit pueblos almost certainly demonstrated two social divisions..." (Lekson 37-38).

Furthermore, Lekson also believes that the Great Houses were built to be expressively ornate, for the purposes of honoring the elite (ala The Vatican?).

Another suggestion that Lekson has offered speculates that the model of elite members supported by a larger community also fits with the political course of ancient times. Lekson argues that those who view Chaco as anything other than a common Mesoamerican political structure are misled, as the altepetl was practiced throughout the southwest during the prime of Chaco. This structure is politically antithetical to the current political structure of the descendants of the Anasazi Chacoans, and therefore, Lekson admits that there are disagreements.

When viewed through the lens of a 2,000year timeline, it is possible modern Pueblo descendants structure their post-Chaco society as a rejection of the Chaco model. Therefore, Lekson does not dispute disseminated descendants; he only disputes the idea that the political structure is the same as it has always been, a model known as an *altepetl*. An altepetl (a Nahua or Aztec term) is a family of elite rulers who preside over commoners who live in the region and appears to have originated in western Mexico. Because of this, the structure of the society is that of a sociopolitical allegiance. There would have been multiple noble families, *tecallis*, and the central ruler would have been an elected member of one of the tecalli. Because of this, the altepetl model would have been one in which nobility would not have passed on as dynasty from genetic lineage, but rather from a vote of the elite tecallis.

In Chaco, the altepetl model of political structure is possibly revealed in the physical layout of the Great Houses, as they were places that would not have been inhabited by commoners.

Not only would commoners *not* have occupied the Great Houses, they would have also served the more elite tecalli who led their altepetl, according to Lekson. Other things that would have been supplied by commoners were baskets, woven goods, pottery, food, and game. And the clan, itself, would have been responsible for specific duties to the tecallis. Everything was a clearly defined hierarchy.

What inspired this change in social and political structure? There was clearly outside influence, either over time or in a quick burst. The construction of intimidating Great Houses may have had the effect (intentionally or unintentionally) of influencing the traders that visited Chaco. There is extensive evidence of a trade network between the Chacoan sphere of influence and Mesoamerica. A trader arriving at Pueblo Bonito would surely have a different opinion of the Chacoans than one arriving at a pit-house to negotiate a deal.

It also makes sense that the Great Houses of downtown Chaco would be built in such close proximity to each other. We assume Pueblo Bonito was the most important of the Great Houses, but neither Chetro Ketl nor Pueblo del Arroyo take a back seat. Consider that Chetro Ketl has more square footage than Pueblo Bonito, and Pueblo del Arroyo is unique for its location near Chaco Wash (with a direct view of the South Gap) rather than under the northern cliffs. With Lekson's theory, the tecalli ruler would live central with other tecallis. From this central point the municipalities of these tecallis would reach outward. The diagram of the altepetl *looks* like the physical layout of Chaco Canyon.

An interesting comment made by Lekson during a presentation on this topic to the Arizona Archaeological and Historical Society is that in order to understand Chaco, we cannot attribute the modern descendant to the Anasazi. The Anasazi did not seek out to *become* Puebloan. It is possible that the Puebloan history, of peace and egalitarianism, evolved after a highly hierarchal society of altepeme became corrupted.

> *"Some believe Chaco represents one of the best North American examples of the evolution of chiefly societies based on institutionalized leadership with significant status differentiation; in contrast, others suggest Chaco was egalitarian, and the massive construction was a cooperative effort coordinated by ephemeral leaders with minimal power. Some have proposed the Great Houses were populous communities comparable with historic pueblos, whereas others argue that they had*

51

a small resident population that was seasonally supplemented by hundreds, if not thousands, of pilgrims who flocked to the canyon for ceremonies and ritual festivals." (Plog and Heitman).

Regardless of the number of inhabitants of Chaco Canyon, any hardy souls who braved the winters in this inhospitable land would have needed clothing, blankets, shelter, and heat to survive. It makes sense this would mean a fire within a room, with clothing and blankets wrapped around the body. The fire would serve double duty for cooking.

A strangeness comes when looking at the number of hearths found in the Great Houses, which is remarkably few. Thomas Windes is credited with using the number of hearths found to estimate population, with the assumption fire was required for sufficient heat to survive in the rooms of the Great Houses. "Rather than focusing on mere numbers of rooms, he chose...fire pits. The fire pit, he reasoned, is a universal necessity for permanent occupation." (Fagan 155).

Is Windes' assumption incorrect? Or is it possible the Great Houses themselves provided adequate thermal protection, even without an on-going fire?

Perhaps these inhabitants were simply tougher than we can imagine, and so well adapted to their environment that our modern minds cannot conceive they could stay warm enough through frigid winters without the heat of a

Kyle Widner

fire. Is it possible that thick piles of blankets, the combined body heat of a family unit, and domesticated dogs curled up as further insulation was sufficient to make it through the coldest of nights?

Many Great House rooms were either not designed or constructed in a way that would allow a fire to be built. Researchers have attempted to build fires in these rooms only to discover the fire snuffs out on its own due to lack of oxygen. Additionally, anyone trying to sustain a fire would have died of gradual carbon monoxide poisoning, as the ventilation would have been inadequate even if a fire could be kept burning.

The Great Houses also function thermodynamically, with each building acting as a solar recipient. G.B. Cornucopia points out that during the coldest part of winter, when the sun is at its lowest point in the sky, Pueblo Bonito receives more solar energy than it would during any other time of the year. Cornucopia also mentioned that a study was performed that measured the *outside* temperature of the walls with a variant of 32°; however, the *inside* temperature of the same wall remained within 1° of variability. This suggests a strong insulation quality in the architecture and masonry of the Great Houses.

Besides the question of fire and hearths, Wendy Bustard, a Chacoan scholar, shared insight in regards to the scarcity of livable elements present in the architecture of Pueblo Bonito: "Built-in mealing bins were non-existent in the sampled rooms, fire pits, small storage facilities, and platforms were present, *but rare*. Rooms with no floor features overwhelm the sample…" (Bustard 90).

Combining the research, there has been compelling factual evidence that the Great Houses were not densely populated. This adds to the mysteries of Chaco: why was so much energy and resources expended to build these magnificent structures, if they were not meant to be used for their obvious purpose?

If the higher estimates of Chacoan population were accurate, we would expect to find an extensive graveyard or ceremonial pyre area. In fact, there have been relatively few burials found in Chaco Canyon, about 300 total. This archaeological quandary suggests that the population was not immense and / or the population was not permanent. The lack of burials, but the high density of "goods" (turquoise, ceramics, wood, etc.) supports the theories of Chaco Canyon as a hub for cultural trade and religious ceremonies.

To further support the notion that there was a low population density is the lack of biological waste in the refuse mounds that are located nearby all the Great Houses. Common to Anasazi existence was the "midden", a trash pile normally located in front of residences. These middens are archeological gold, layers and layers of refuse, broken pots, deteriorated baskets, broken tools, food waste, animal bones and carcasses, all arranged in chronological order, oldest on the bottom, newest on the top. Examination of the mounds at the Great Houses was expected to yield such results, as they have in countless Anasazi sites. But, in yet another Chacoan surprise, little in the way of household waste was found. This is further evidence of a paucity of permanent population in the Great Houses. The mounds that were expected to yield a rich record of daily Chacoan life were comprised mainly of discarded construction materials.

Even amongst the most learned scholars of Chaco Canyon, population estimates have varied widely:

> *"With a margin for error, it has been estimated that Pueblo Bonito once numbered eight hundred rooms. A few score of these rooms would either have been abandoned or used only for storage, making it unlikely that more than one thousand persons ever lived in Bonito at one time."* (McNitt 129).

> *"...the chronological reconstruction of Pueblo Bonito suggests that the population never exceeded 100 people..."* (Windes 32).

Wesley Bernardini, another prominent Chacoan scholar, calculates that 70 people occupied Pueblo Bonito, and 200 rooms were used exclusively for storage; (Fagan 140).

> *"An estimated 5000 to 6000 people lived in the vicinity of Chaco Canyon..."* (Lister and Lister 197).

Or:

Kyle Widner

"A small number of people, hundreds at most, lived in Chaco Canyon Great Houses...however, I estimate that the population of Chaco's greater region was perhaps twice that of the San Juan Basin; that is, something under 100,000..." (Lekson 11).

Or:

"No one will ever know how many pueblos were occupied at the peak of Chaco's golden period...Some have estimated the population to have been ten thousand, but that is no more than a guess." (McNitt 129).

To answer the enigmatic question of actual population of Chaco Canyon:

"Archaeologists have arrived at dramatically different population estimates for Chaco Canyon from A.D. 850 to 1150..." (Vivian and Hilpert 217).

Again, all this leaves us with a head-scratching puzzle missing many pieces. There was a population that lived there, but the ratio of Great Houses and rooms to the few number of burials and large quantity of trade and ceremonial goods is completely out of whack with what we would expect to find. Independent of the actual population number, it seems clear there was a social hierarchy not seen in previous manifestations of Anasazi civilization, or the resultant Puebloan societies.

Daily Life in Chaco Canyon

The vast majority of books written on Chaco Canyon have been timeline based, that is, they cover the rise, florescence, and decline of the Chaco phenomenon. Not as much has been written about the daily existence of a Chacoan, going about their life. Perhaps the first attempt to unravel this part of the mystery was the seminal article in National Geographic Magazine of September 1925, Everyday Life in Pueblo Bonito, by Neil M. Judd. Since then, countless research studies, archaeological excavations, and technological improvements have updated and expanded upon Judd's work.

Human nature features common elements that transcend time and geography. Often, as we study ancient cultures, the people themselves become more "concept" than human, and we lose our connection to them. The Chacoans likely had the same hopes, desires, feelings, and emotions as modern citizens of the world, but expressed these things in a way consistent with their societal norms.

According to the National Park Service: "Like us, Chacoans needed food and water containers, building and hunting tools, and clothing. They used fire starters, awls and needles, and cordage to make life easier. Pipes, gaming pieces, and effigy figurines made leisure time more pleasurable. Indeed, as there is a Chacoan mystery, it is instructive to remember that the Anasazi did not construct this puzzle for our modern marvel. *We* have created the mystery of Chaco. Daily existence was not a mystery for the Anasazi, and they certainly felt no need to leave any

57

conclusive archaeological clues for us. The Anasazi did not build these structures for our interpretation. The Anasazi were not practical jokers, plotting the longest prank in archaeological history: *The Mystery of Chaco*."

Daily life in Chaco likely had elements much like our own; navigating the obstacles of basic existence, filling leisure time, and all without consideration for the ease of future archaeological study. This would have included feelings of love for and the desire to protect their family, the passion they would have for one's lover, and the fear of one's enemy.

Stephen Lekson proposed a controversial theory concerning the social structure of the Chacoans. In this theory, he suggests that Chaco Canyon was one of the most powerful altepeme of all time. Furthermore, Lekson argues that if this was the predominant structure of the ancient southwest, Chaco Canyon would be "Exhibit A" in way of evidence.

As referenced earlier, Lekson's view is that the Great Houses were homes for the altepeme's elite families. The daily routine of a Chacoan would vary greatly, given his place within his altepetl. According to Dr. Laurel Cooper:

> *"Anomalies like the paucity of burials and the presence of elite goods caused a reevaluation of the role of great houses during the extensive research program of the Chaco Centre. It emphasized a*

redistribution model, with a managerial elite living in the great houses and controlling goods stored in the now-empty suites..." (Cooper 22-23).

The flip side of this theory is one of a self-contained, peaceful society, where there would have been no formal social structure, per se, but clans would have had specific duties to perform in order to support the whole. Under this theory, the people of Chaco would have been self-regulating, self-reliant, and disciplined. Anecdotally, this appears to be the model the modern Pueblo (descendant of the Anasazi) peoples adhere to.

While utopian in nature, the aforementioned theory seems unlikely. The massive organized effort to construct Great Houses alone seems to discredit it, given the exponential technological boom from basic pit-house structures to complex, multi-story dwellings. This construction effort would have required a hierarchy of highly skilled and knowledgeable individuals who controlled and directed the project, which begs the question: what was the organization or hierarchy?

There are multiple conflicting theories as to the form of the hierarchy, with some even arguing there was no hierarchy at all. Even less believable are theories suggesting that the labor force might have been a team of only 16 men. To put the common sense absurdity of this into context, could you believe a team of 16 could have built a 4 story Great House the size of the Roman Coliseum? Only 16 people to mine, quarry, shape, and

59

import the stones, make the mortar, cut down the massive logs required for support beams, trim and shape them, carry them from more than 50 miles away, and assemble a 4 story building? And with no metal tools, written language, the wheel, or draft animals?

While we don't understand the structure of society in terms of building the Great Houses, on the domestic side, if we take the imprint of known, modern Puebloan culture, and extrapolate backwards, we can surmise some elements of familial organization. The domestic structure of the Chacoan household was likely matrilineal. Therefore, when a husband married into the clan, the husband would reside in the wife's home, partake in the wife's family's practices, and provide food for the household.

Neil Judd, during his 1924 excavation, writes of the domestic duties of the woman as:

> *"In prehistoric Bonito there existed a curious division of domestic responsibility. 'Woman's Rights' were already recognized and in vogue. The head of the Bonitian household was the wife and mother, not the husband. Times have changed since then, but history tends always to repeat itself!"*(Judd 233).

Judd goes on to describe the daily life of the Chacoans:

> *"Family life in Pueblo Bonito probably differed very little from...[modern western*

Pueblos]...Descent was unquestioningly matrilineal, the mother, rather than the father was the head of the household. Married daughters, with their husbands and children would continue to live in the matrilineal home. All shared the same living quarters, same hearth, and kitchen utensils. Meals were eaten twice a day from food bowls placed directly upon the floor; fingers served in lieu of forks. Blankets and pelts were folded during the day, and spread on the floor at night." (Judd; Frazier 50).

During the warmer months, the clothing of the Chacoans was primarily loin cloths made out of yucca fiber or cotton-like materials. Intricately woven sandals made of yucca have been excavated, along with stockings or leggings of fibers. Robes of warm feathers, skins and textiles have also been found, possibly used during the colder months; (Lister and Lister 54).

Some have postulated that the "shelves" found within the architecture of the Great Houses might actually have been beds; however, it is more likely that they would lay down on the floor in piles of sheep's skin and rabbit's fur, wrapped in woven blankets. As Judd describes:

"Tanned skins and blankets of rabbit fur, neatly piled to one side during the day, were spread out on the bare floor as beds at night. A tuft of eagle feathers, suspended from the ceiling, protected the household

Kyle Widner

from evil spirits, as it swayed gently with the soft movement of air through the rooms." (Judd 252).

Judd found evidence of clothes racks, as well, which would have housed additional clothing and blankets. There has been little evidence of furniture excavated; the existence of a solitary stool being the most furniture present in many rooms. It has been noted that furniture is not a priority in modern descendant's homes; therefore, the paucity of furniture does not imply scarce habitation.

In Judd's opinion, beds were likely to be padded with additional daytime clothing made of cotton, turkey feather robes, and tanned hides; (Frazier 51). A turkey-feather blanket that was even a few inches thick would have offered substantial insulation against the cold. Families most likely shared sleeping accommodations to generate body heat.

The average Chacoan likely would have awoken as the sun rose, keen observers of sunrises and sunsets. Knowledge of agriculture would have had to be related to knowledge of the seasonal moons and sun positioning.

There is evidence children began "on the job" training at a young age. One example is found in the clay that was used to make the exquisite pottery of Chaco. Excavated ceramic pottery has been discovered with children's tiny ancient fingerprints; indelible upon the pots they created. In a society without a known written language, training by practice, combined with oral tradition and story-telling would have insured continuity and the passing of accumulated knowledge.

Judd speculates that children might have counted and recounted stones as form of entertainment—an interesting theory that helps us grasp the notion of mathematics in Ancient Chaco. Small items, thought to be game pieces, have been found. It is hard to conceive of a game with pieces that would not involve some sort of basic arithmetic.

If we expand upon the pottery-making example, we can assume the children would have begun learning their adult duties and roles from an early age, but play would also have been important. Items likely to be toys have been found. Neil Judd speculates from his 1924 excavations that the children probably played with coyote pups, their own puppies, as the Chacoans had domesticated dogs, and were likely infatuated with birds that were caged, such as macaws and eagles. At the time, domesticated turkeys ran free range in the area, and it isn't hard to imagine Chacoan children chasing them much as children would later chase chickens.

More than pets, domesticated dogs would have been helpful as watchdogs and during chilly nights, serving to provide some welcome body heat. Possibly, although no evidence exists, dogs were a part of hunting efforts.

As for childhood in Chaco Canyon: it was short. The Anasazi rarely lived much past thirty years old. By age twenty-nine, one would be an elder with osteoarthritis.

Childbearing ages had to be relatively young, probably as soon as puberty allowed. A harsh reality, but not uncommon in ancient civilizations.

Whereas the men hunted for food, food preparation was the responsibility of the young Chacoan women. This preparation involved understanding the proper storage and cooking methods, as well as providing social opportunities. Gossip likely existed then; just as it does now, further evidence of the human nature of people. Young women would obviously be conversing while working corn over their metates (corn grinding stones). Neil Judd speculates that: "…while precious yellow kernels were being crunched between the milling stones, black-eyed maidens shyly gossiped of promising village swains or sang…" (235).

Working the mano (hand held stone to grind corn in the metate) incessantly to grind corn was daily, repetitive, boring work. It is not hard to imagine these ladies giggling with stories, gossiping, and perhaps singing work songs as a brace against the monotony.

These well-worn manos and metates are still commonly found in Anasazi ruins, although the metate is normally broken in ritual fashion when the occupants leave, for unknown reasons. There exists today a large metate in the Pueblo Bonito ruin in Chaco.

Metate and mano: a common find at Anasazi ruins. This tool was used for grinding corn.

In the Chacoan civilization, everyone had a job to do, usually dependent on clan or familial affiliation. Young boys would follow their fathers on hunting trips, to the fields to tend crops, or assist in the building of the Great Houses. They would have also been a part of the kiva ceremonies; kivas are specialized structures, circular, underground rooms commonly thought to have been used for ceremonies, as the Hopi and other Anasazi descendants continue to do today. While it is impossible to know with certainty, kivas were also likely used for passing oral tradition, training, community meetings, and as workspaces during cold periods.

Each Anasazi household served a specific function within the clan, as Judd observed:

"The daily struggle for existence was paramount then as now, and each inhabitant

65

of the village, old and young alike, necessarily contributed his share to the support of the community as a whole." (Judd 231).

And Fagan documented:

"Households farmed the land, gathered plant foods, and hunted. Their members prepared food, manufactured pots and weapons, built houses, and fashioned ornaments. Each family and household was an autonomous unit; each organized its annual work cycle." (Fagan 145).

For the average "housewife" the chores and work would have been never-ending. Judd states:

"Housewives pursued their daily task out of doors when possible—making pottery, preparing food, tending babies, etc.—on the terraced rooftops or in the courtyards below. Naked children romped, like happy puppies, all over the place..." (Judd: Frazier 51).

This halcyon view of Chaco Canyon is inviting and further lends to a conclusion of Chaco as a peaceful, productive society.

Weapons crafted for military-style purposes are rarely found during excavations, further supporting this view. Without the need for a standing army, the Chaco people were free to dedicate themselves as woodworkers, stone masons, hunters, and farmers. Stone tools, planting sticks, axes, trowels, hammers, knives, and wedges have been excavated in abundance.

Theories of warfare and siege have been postulated, mostly based on the "sealing" of Great House doors and windows. However, as more information has become available via scientific methods and archaeological interpretation, these theories do not hold up. The doors and windows were carefully, deliberately, sealed over the course of a generation, prior to migration. This, combined with a lack of weapons, is not what we would expect to find if a siege or other wartime period descended over Chaco, necessitating a rapid retreat.

However, it is hard to believe a society that lasted as long as the Chaco phenomenon not escaping conflict at some stage. It is easy to imagine the strategic location of some of the Great Houses and related structures allowed them to serve as sentinels or lookouts. The fact that Pueblo Bonito's walls were increasingly made secure also suggests that the residents perceived external threats, which could explain the single gateway to Pueblo Bonito. Access to many of the rooms of the Great Houses was gained only by ladder, instead of a ground level entrance; ladders are easily pulled up to the rooftop to prevent invaders from gaining entry. By considering the disadvantages of ground level occupation versus the advantages of being elevated, it could explain the multi-story structures, even when there was plentiful land. Building upwards instead of outwards

Kyle Widner

may have been itself a defensive one, and could provide the elite both protection and a visual advantage.

Absent warfare or threat of raiders, much of the population would have been preparing goods to trade as a daily occupation and there would have been open plazas to conduct bartering and commerce. Paul Reed describes trade in Chaco vividly:

"Among the goods we can envision trading hands were ceramic vessels from the Chuska Valley and elsewhere, high quality stone raw materials, such as Narbona Pass chert and Jemez Mountains obsidian, carefully woven cotton textiles and yucca sandals, and perhaps some exotic items such as live macaws from Mexico, and beautifully crafted jewelry of turquoise, shell, jet, and other luxuriant materials." (Reed 79).

Yucca sandal and pottery: a remnant of a yucca cord sandal, pieces of pottery, and an antler found near a cave in southeast Utah.

Turquoise dominated the marketplace at Chaco and much effort was dedicated to refining turquoise into tools and art pieces. Exquisite flesher tools have been found, decorated with turquoise bands. The tiny jet frog featured in the National Park Service Visitor's Guide could not have been machined in today's world to be any more perfect than it is. It is clear the Anasazi appreciated art and craftsmanship, showing perfectionism and impeccable detail in both their architecture and art.

Out of all art forms at Chaco, pottery is the most ubiquitous. Some pottery was definitely made in Chaco, but others believe most of the ceramic wares were imported, and perhaps finished turquoise was provided as payment. The archaeological record supports the imported conclusion; with a large percentage of the pottery sherds

69

excavated indicating creation in other locations. With wood for fire at such a premium, it is easy to imagine a decision to conserve wood for warmth and cooking, versus using it for creating something that could be easily imported.

Exquisitely decorated Anasazi pottery (some complete specimens, but mostly in sherds) survives, and exists today. In fact, sherds are still easily spotted around most Anasazi ruins, including Una Vida and Peñasco Blanco in Chaco. The care and attention to detail of the colors and patterns is impeccable, and the creators obviously took great pride in their work. The colors survive, mineral paints made bright with high iron content and rich blacks created from boiled bee weed and tansy mustard plants. Paint brushes created from yucca fibers and held in well practiced hands stroked precise lines and geometric patterns. Judd, after years of examining thousands of examples, exclaimed the Chacoans had elevated pottery to fine art.

Spotting and examining an Anasazi pottery sherd with these precise patterns stirs the imagination. Knowing that nearly a thousand years ago another human being created this art and it rests here, untouched for a millennium or more is a connection across time, which cannot be adequately explained in words.

Women wore make-up and jewelry, much as they do now. Jewelry, in the form of necklaces and pendants were common. Earrings have been found that match necklaces. Some of the adornments are incredibly ornate, consider one necklace Judd located; it featured over 2500 individually crafted turquoise beads. Judd observed that it is likely that the women also applied rouge to their cheeks, easily obtainable from minerals in the surrounding red rocks. The notion of Ancient make-up and jewelry is intriguing to some, but certainly humanizing. These Chacoans had egos, and aesthetic appreciation. Judd believed that the necklace was prized in its own time and rare, for he thought it had been hidden to protect it from marauders. The necklace was found in the northern end of room 320 in Pueblo Bonito, between two pieces of flagstone. The necklace had been purposefully coiled and contained the earrings in its center. The ancient person who hid it did so purposefully, and covered it with mud and ashes; (Frazier 52).

It would be wonderful to transport back to that moment and know, exactly, why that necklace was hidden so carefully, and by whom. Clearly, this necklace was a treasure in its own time, and it may very well be one of the most amazing archaeological finds of Judd's expedition.

Finds such as the necklace and other artifacts indicate turquoise was highly valued, and likely a prized currency in trade. While turquoise does not exist naturally in Chaco Canyon itself, many believe that turquoise came from nearby mines, such as the one in Guadalupe, which still produces to this day. Based on the archeological record, it is clear this semi-precious stone was a central component of Chacoan life.

One thing we can never know with certainty is the sounds of the canyon, especially the music. Flutes have been excavated, such as the highly ornate flute from Room 33; (Pepper 166), which also held a rare shell trumpet. It is known that shell bells existed even before copper bells. Drums came in all shapes and sizes. It is likely that the daily life within the Great Houses echoed with the rhythmic sounds of foot drums beating in the underground kivas. There may have been the melody of the flute mingling with the pounding of the drum, chanting, and singing.

Small copper bells were likely imported from Mexico, as the Anasazi did not craft with metal. These were likely banded around dancers' ankles and wrists in order to connect the dancer to the music. It is only natural to interpret the music, dances, and singing of the modern Puebloan tribes as descending from these Anasazi rites, but tantalizingly, we can never know for sure.

There is much to contemplate when thinking of daily life in Chaco, 1000 years ago. As modern visitors, we experience only a slice of time in Chaco, of a few days, at most. We wear comfortable shoes, wrap ourselves in clothing designed to protect us from heat, cold, or wind, all the while sipping fresh water from sealed bottles and unwrapping energy bars, or snacking on nuts from California.

Despite the harshness of their existence, the Anasazi took time to create and appreciate beauty, in their tools, jewelry, even the detail they placed in their masonry. Reconciling the attention to beauty and day-to-day challenges of life in this environment is fodder for an active imagination.

Evolution of Chacoan Masonry and Architecture

"Architecture is an area in which elite individuals or institutions express their power; from palaces and pyramids to roads and temples. This is done in two ways: either through the sheer impressiveness of the finished product, or through the sheer impressiveness of the amount of labor required to construct the finished product." (Metcalf 73).

Viewing the Great Houses from the perspective listed above, it is possible that the entire purpose of these buildings was solely to *build* them.

Part of the mystique of Chaco Canyon is the riddle of understanding how knowledge was passed down from generation to generation without a written language. It is possible that there was a written record recorded on clay or some other medium that has not survived the test of time and the elements. But this possibility is remote enough that it is universally discarded. There was clearly a high level understanding of architecture, engineering, building, and masonry, which spanned nearly a dozen generations, and this knowledge was obviously passed on.

We're left to assume the knowledge would have been passed as an oral tradition, recorded in the minds of each generation, who would then instill specific knowledge in the next generation. This would have required incredible memory and repetition, as well as attention to the most minute of details. Were geometric equations drawn in the sand, and wiped away at the end of each session, as the Freemasons of Europe did when schooling illiterate apprentices?

By breaking down the needed skills into specialties, it would minimize how much one person would have to know and memorize. But someone, or some class of person, would have to know how all the specialties fit together. And as improvements to techniques were made, technology introduced, or new materials discovered, this too, would have to be incorporated in the knowledge passed on. Perhaps that is why there are so many kivas, serving as classrooms and teaching centers. It seems logical this process would have begun at a young age, apprentices learning the basics as soon as their minds were able to grasp the concepts.

These learned individuals would possibly serve as the foremen, as well, guiding a team of workers highly skilled and practiced in masonry and construction. The precise nature of the massive Great Houses is proof that however they did it, they were very, very good at it. As we would expect, each generation likely improved upon the work of the last. And, consistent with human nature, they added their own flair or style. When looking closely at the remaining masonry at Chaco, one can clearly discern with the naked eye aesthetic distinctions between eras.

Chacoan architecture and stonework displays generational shifts and observable transitions between phases of stonework. These phases are intriguing both architecturally and anthropologically. The idea that each generation rebels against the last generation is not a new story. There is something *humanizing* about the obvious modifications in the construction efforts of one generation to the next.

Architecture is inexorably linked to the materials available and used. The Chacoan Great House builders had very limited choices. They had a selection of locally available stones, timbers which had to be imported from 50+ miles away, and a rudimentary type of mortar / concrete called adobe. In Judd's account of the use of adobe in Chaco Canyon, he explains how adobe was made: "They gather a great pile of twigs of thyme (sagebrush) and sedge grass, and set it afire, and when its half coals and ashes they throw a quantity of dirt and water on it and mix it all up." The combination of vegetal material would have added strength and rigidity to the adobe, which would have been important, as that was what was used to mortar the stones in place. It has obviously worked well, judging from its longevity.

The progression that led up to the advanced architectural knowledge that the Anasazi mastered commenced in their nomadic Basketmaker Era roots. The progression from the Basketmaker Eras to Pueblo III Period is illustrated by leading Chaco archaeological scholar Stephen Lekson. He presents this progression and the technologies associated with each step:

Basketmaker I Era: corn

Basketmaker II Era: pottery + corn

Pueblo I Period: stone masonry + pottery + corn

Pueblo II Period: kivas + stone masonry + pottery + corn

Pueblo III Period: mass pueblos + kivas + stone masonry + pottery + corn

In order to understand these different masonry styles and stonework, the periods of Puebloan florescence within Chaco Canyon are divided as follows:

Pueblo I Period: 750-900 AD

Pueblo II Period: 900-1150 AD (Bonito Phase and Golden Age of Chaco)

Pueblo III Period: 1150-1350 AD

The construction that remains from Pueblo I builders' shows that the tools and techniques used to refine individual stones was not yet perfected. The stones are uneven and project at uneven angles. In fact, the finished side of the wall looks similar to a chunk of exposed core and veneer internal workings. While rough, one can clearly see the seeds of the architectural magnificence to come:

"It's easy to identify the stonework of the earliest masons, as it appears crude and rudimentary in comparison with the advanced masonry that followed. The walls were simple, single rows of masonry set in

76

adobe mortar and the builders needed extra reinforcement or wall-strength, therefore they would erect a second wall, but did not ever fill the gap between the two walls." (Fagan 119).

The second generation, Pueblo II, displays uniform and sequentially aligned stonework, usually alternating little stones with large stones in symmetrical rows, possibly functional, but likely a mark of craftsmanship or pride. In the final phase of Pueblo II and III Periods we find the McElmo type of masonry, which is a more contemporary style ala brick work, featuring symmetrical large rocks more often than small intricate stonework. One theory is the abrupt disparity between McElmo and Bonito or Hosta Butte phases is due to outside influence. This progression through the three time periods is evident to the naked eye in the ruins that remain today in Chaco.

Masonry in the Pueblo II Period is distinct due to the tightly stacked narrow stones, mostly flat and strikingly uniform in size. These small slat stones evolve into the subsequent generations' use of slat stones and round stones with an alternating pattern. These exquisitely crafted stones have highly precise 90° angles, no small feat without the use of geometry or tools.

As the Pueblo II Period unfolded, the focus continued on the construction of the original three Great Houses, and commenced on the building of Kin Nahasbas and Hungo Pavi, and finally, in the latest part of the period, Chetro Ketl and Pueblo Alto. Sound, proven construction techniques, both architecturally and structurally, are a mark of this period. The Pueblo II builders were steadily learning and improving upon what already existed.

According to Lekson, the three phases can be differentiated as such:

> *"The salient characteristics distinguishing McElmo sites from (as identified by Vivian and Mathews) from Hosta Butte and Bonito sites are their site plans, their masonry styles, their late dates…and their status as new construction rather than rebuilding or remodeling of existing structures."* (Sebastian 30).

In Great House architecture, such as Pueblo Bonito, it is clear that there are multiple generations at work. A worker that began young, in the early days of the construction of Pueblo Bonito, did not live to see its completion. The science of dendrochronology (tree-ring dating) has taken much of the guesswork out the beginning and end construction dates. The massive logs used as beams in the Great Houses can be accurately dated to the year they were cut down. One wrinkle that occasionally appears is the Chacoan tendency to remodel, and recycle building materials from past projects. Taking this into consideration, archaeologists work with a high degree of confidence when they discuss dates of construction in Chaco Canyon.

Kyle Widner

As one views the intricate stonework of these Great Houses, it is hard to imagine that the stonework was *not* the finished exterior feature. A layer of plaster was applied, or the walls were whitewashed:

> *"For whitewash, the people had used a soft-muddy looking sandstone...Judd and his colleagues did an experiment and learned that [the sandstone] readily disintegrates in water 'and produces a grayish pigment identical in all outward appearances with that employed by the ancients."* (Judd; Frazier 50).

The intricate masonry seems to be a facade of achievement in and of itself. If the walls were indeed whitewashed, then all of the intricate stonework that awes the modern visitor was not visible to the contemporary Chacoan from 850-1150. Neil Judd and his excavators discovered that the whitewash that the Chacoans used was made of sandstone and applied as a thin coat of plaster for the walls. Imagining the magnificence of Pueblo Bonito whitewashed is difficult. Plus, we'll never know what type of art or images may have been displayed on this whitewash, if any.

In Pueblo Bonito alone, there are sub-categories to the time periods that can be broken down into five different masonry and veneer styles.

> *"These styles vary in the kind of stones used and in the ways they are arranged. Early*

Kyle Widner

*styles favored hard, dark brown sandstone
of uniform size. Later styles used
multicolored, softer, tabular stones of
greater size and variability. The latest style
often incorporated large, soft, yellowish
blocks, often ground smooth on the exposed
surface."* (Neitzel 15).

Both the small houses and Great Houses are
constructed out of intricate masonry, adobe, and timber.
The timber added a degree of flexibility to the structures,
which has likely contributed to helping the buildings resist
the literal sands of time. According to Brian Fagan, these
structures would have had as much as forty tons of stone in
one single room.

Three Great Houses (Pueblo Bonito, Una Vida, and
Peñasco Blanco) are credited with being the first
constructed in Chaco Canyon:

*"They made three buildings large, multi-
storied, and arc-shaped (except for a dog-
leg at Una Vida mandated by topography).
They gave them all remarkably similar floor
plans. They created a line of large circular
pit structures in the plaza. Behind them they
built a row of large ramada-living rooms, a
second row of large featureless rooms, and
in the rear a third row of smaller storage
rooms."* (Frazier 175).

Architecturally, there are numerous similarities between the Great Houses. They have ubiquitous windows and doorways that would have required significant forethought and planning to allow for proper alignment. An intriguing fact about core and veneer masonry is that it is *unique* to Chaco Canyon, and not found elsewhere in the San Juan Basin prior to Chaco. It is possible that this knowledge and technology was not imported but developed in Chaco Canyon to address the needs of their multistory architecture; (Fagan 120).

G.B. Cornucopia explains how the veneer was made up of rocks that were chipped from the surrounding sandstone; it cleaves naturally into flat 90° angles. This cleavage made it easy to manipulate and the perfect stone for polished veneer masonry. The core of the wall would be comprised of similar unfinished stone that had been extracted from the same geological level as the veneer. The Chacoans understood rock density and understood that in order to build successfully, densities must remain even throughout construction. This form of core and veneer also created the first "insulation", which we know of. As previously mentioned, it proved effective, as there is only a 1° variance between the room and wall temperature inside the structures. These improvements were for more than just structural support alone.

According to R. Gwinn Vivian and Bruce Hilpert's, *The Chaco Handbook* (50-53), Pueblo Bonito was the first Great House under construction, and for unknown reasons its building was halted for a short phase while Una Vida was built. Then the construction of Una Vida halted whilst

81

the construction on both Pueblo Bonito and Peñasco Blanco increased. There is an eighty-year period that appears dormant from dendrochronology: "Following this early triad...the Chacoans may have taken an eighty-year hiatus. Generations came and went with little significant new construction." (Frazier 176). Again, with most things Chaco, we can speculate, but the reasons remain a mystery.

Concerning the layout of the earliest construction within the canyon as a whole: Una Vida is the easternmost Great House in the canyon proper, with a view of Fajada Butte to the southeast. Una Vida is the first Great House located on the right hand drive of the present-day one-way loop. Pueblo Bonito is roughly 3 miles from Una Vida on the loop drive, and it is the largest of the ruins. One must park at the Pueblo del Arroyo parking lot and commence a 3 mile hike to the canyon's outermost edge in order to view Peñasco Blanco. Therefore, the earliest construction is well-spaced throughout the canyon, for several Great Houses are all approximately 3 miles apart. Whether this is a coincidence, or an intentional part of a bigger plan is unknown.

These external buildings permitted communication and offer views of far off mesas, such as Hosta Butte, the San Mateo Mountains, the Continental Divide, and Escavada Wash. Because of this, Ancient Chacoans were able to keep diligent watch on the surrounding topography, whilst nurturing a safe homestead in Pueblo Bonito. Additionally, the location of these buildings suggests that water could be had from the confluence of major washes at both ends of the canyon.

Scattered throughout the canyon are numerous smaller houses, constructed with similar but rougher techniques. It is theorized that these are the homes of workers or laborers. Or, if Chaco was not occupied full time as some have suggested, perhaps they were transient housing for traders and visitors. These smaller houses, in combination with the traditional pit-houses, could have housed construction and support crews. One of the earliest sites of these smaller pueblos is referred to as the Three-C Site, discovered by Gordon Vivian near a camp built by the Civilian Conservation Corps, and located at the base of Fajada Butte. The Three-C Site has not been dated by dendrochronology, but ceramics and the trash mound (midden), along with burials, suggest that the site was occupied between 870-950. This occupation would have been concurrent with the construction of Pueblo Bonito; (Vivian and Hilpert 263).

Sixteen burials have been found at the Three-C site, a surprisingly high number for a smaller site when compared to other areas of the canyon.

> *"The Three-C Site...was a unit-type pueblo, was occupied in the tenth century (perhaps even before), and the number of rooms, two kivas, and sixteen burials found there indicate that it may have housed three families over a considerable amount of time."* (McNitt 127).

The masonry and architecture of Chaco are the dominant features of the canyon. Walking among the majestic ruins inspires awe and by now, the all too common questions. The sheer scope and scale, the precision, and the beauty in design clearly define the Chacoans as skilled architects and masons. Even today, the Great Houses they constructed command attention and admiration, built with skills honed over hundreds of years, a 1000+ years ago.

Pueblo Bonito: The Greatest Great House

The Great Houses are what make Chaco Canyon unique. These grand monuments to human ingenuity and engineering represent ancient organization on a massive scale. The smaller houses and buildings in the canyon, though archaeologically interesting, are not uncommon in the Anasazi world. Something different, something special happened here, and Pueblo Bonito represents the crown jewel of this fluorescence.

Synonymous with Chaco Canyon, Pueblo Bonito is the most famous of the Great Houses, and despite a century of study focused on it, continues to generate more questions than answers. Tree ring data suggests it was built over a 200year span (860-1080 AD), which explains architectural differences and styles, but little else.

Pueblo Bonito is centrally located within a grouping of other Great Houses, including Chetro Ketl, Kin Kletso and Pueblo del Arroyo, an area commonly referred to as "downtown Chaco". The footprint of Pueblo Bonito is a distinctive "D" shape, containing more than 300 ground floor rooms, 32 kivas, and 3 Great Kivas. According to respected scholar Jill Neitzel:

> *"An enormous building, Pueblo Bonito rose four stories tall, held perhaps as many as 800 total rooms, and encompassed almost three acres."* (Neitzel I).

Two large, intriguing mounds in front of Pueblo Bonito were expected to yield archaeological gold in the form of chronologically layered household rubbish. But these mounds (middens), typically found at Anasazi ruins, surprised the excavators when they yielded little but construction debris. If this was a Great House, then where was the household trash dump?

But was Pueblo Bonito intended to be inhabited, and if so, by whom, and how many? And regardless of its purpose, why was it built under a dangerous cliff with a large portion ominously poised to come crashing down? If the consensus is that Pueblo Bonito was *not* primarily a residential building, then what was its purpose and function? Perhaps it was a ceremonial center, reserved for rituals and ceremonies. Possibly, Pueblo Bonito was a center for trade and commerce. Fragments of tantalizing evidence hint at possibilities, without delivering any conclusive proof.

"We have a lot of facts, but we can't agree on what Chaco was...there are a staggering range of interpretations [of the Chaco mystery]...But something of an embarrassment: we've been digging around Chaco for over a century, and we have plenty of data, so we should be able to solve that mystery. As archaeologists, that's what we are paid to do." (Lekson 36).

Construction was neither consistent nor linear at Pueblo Bonito; it progressed in fits and starts spanning

Kyle Widner

nearly two centuries, representing many generations of architects and workers. Were these builders part of the same genetic lineage, or were there fluctuating populations moving in and out of the canyon?

> *"Judd felt certain the archaeological evidence pointed to Pueblo Bonito being the product of two distinct groups...Old Bonitians and the Late Bonitians...Judd felt that the Old Bonitians were passive and responsible for the initial construction of Pueblo Bonito. However, Judd viewed the Late Bonitians as aggressive. Judd asserts that the Late Bonitians invited immigrants into the culture and were the primary developers of Pueblo Bonito. He felt the second generation was aggressive as they replaced the dormant structure of the Old Bonitians.* (Frazier 54).

One of the most fascinating finds during the Pueblo Bonito excavations was a collection of larger cylinder shaped mugs. An analysis of the residue that remained in these mugs revealed nearly thousand-year old chocolate! The vessels were unique, confined to a single room, and obviously for special or ceremonial use. They are tall, elongated, and cylindrical, usually with ornate designs. This lends credence to the theory of Pueblo Bonito as the most important center, as cocoa would have been rare and exotic, and was not found anywhere else in the canyon. The presence of cocoa, whose nearest tree is 1200 miles away in Mexico, combined with scarlet macaw skeletons, copper bells, and seashells from the Pacific Ocean, is clear evidence of a wide-ranging trade network.

The choice of location for Pueblo Bonito is an odd one, having been built right at the base of the northern cliff wall, under an unstable geographical feature aptly called "Threatening Rock". This huge section of looming cliff sat on a less than sturdy shale surface. It was obviously a concern for the Chacoans, as they supported it with braces in hopes of keeping it from tumbling down upon them. Interestingly, as Pueblo Bonito grew, the expansion was to the east, even closer to Threatening Rock.

> *"Given the obvious danger should the rock fall, it is possible that the builders deliberately chose to expand the site in this direction because they knew that the structure would eventually be crushed—in other words, was Pueblo Bonito was intended to be a monumental sacrifice? [like] large-scale ritual destruction similar to pottery?"* (Marshall 12).

On January 21, 1941, "Threatening Rock" fulfilled its threat, destroying the northeastern section of Pueblo Bonito, doing more damage in an instant than a thousand years of time and the elements.

Pueblo Bonito's main central wall is perfectly aligned, north to south. At the highest point of the mid-day sun, the shadow on this wall disappears. At first, it might be easy to dismiss this as a coincidence. But further study has

Kyle Widner

shown Chaco architecture to be filled with these solar (and lunar) alignments. In a documentary titled "The Mystery of Chaco Canyon", Anna Sofaer demonstrates that Pueblo Bonito and Chetro Ketl form an east / west alignment that is perfectly bisected by the north / south alignment of Pueblo Alto and Tsin Kletzin. This hardly seems coincidental, even if we cannot fully grasp the reasoning.

Kivas

There is an unmistakable feature of Puebloan architecture that dominates the architecture at Chaco: *kivas*. These round recessed rooms are ubiquitous in Anasazi pueblo ruins. Much of the understanding of the role of the kiva is drawn from the modern descendants of the Anasazi, especially the Hopi. The word "kiva" itself is a Hopi word that refers to modern round rooms in modern pueblos. Kivas are mostly partially recessed below ground level, perfectly round, and are found in many sizes, with the largest class being called Great Kivas.

> *"Kivas are round, subterranean structures with a standardized set of floor features: a shipap or sipapu (a small hole, the symbolic place of origin), a bench, a fire box, a deflector shield, and a ventilator shaft for the intake of fresh air...There is some variation in these features, but a standard variation utilized by the Chacoans was the kiva with radial log pilasters. These pilasters were small masonry boxes that enclosed a beam shallowly anchored in the outer wall of the kiva. They were equally spaced around the perimeter of the bench, usually numbering six in a kiva."* (Heitman 259).

Most kivas, particularly the smaller ones, are accessed by an opening in the top, with a ladder for entering and exiting the subterranean room. In some larger

Kyle Widner

kivas, there is a different entryway, similar to a New York subway entrance, where a stair-like descent could be made. The classic example of this is Casa Rinconada, directly across Chaco Canyon from Pueblo Bonito. One theory is these entryways were the symbolic entry of the Anasazi from the third world to this fourth world. But more likely, ladders were impractical due to the sheer size of the Great Kivas. Depending on the pitch of the roof, it could require a ladder of 40' or more in height.

Casa Rinconada: the greatest of Chaco Canyon's great kivas. This is more than 60' across, and could seat almost 400 for ceremonies and rituals. It had a roof of logs, thatch, and grass, and was accessed from stairways on the north and south sides.

Casa Rinconada's construction commenced about 1070, and continued until 1105 and remains an excellent example of the features of a Great Kiva. It's about 63-64' in diameter and about 20' tall from roof to floor with 34 open niches, 28 forming one encircling series, as 6 larger ones making up a second group; (Lister and Lister 107).

The larger ones are an anomaly, for they are not placed evenly or predictably apart, and for no known reason.

In Casa Rinconada, there is an encircling inner bench; a firebox; 4 pits to hold support beams for the roof frame; raised masonry vaults or foot drums; and small niches built into the inner wall, presumably for holding ritual objects; (Vivian and Hilpert 80). This place differs from the other excavated Great Kivas because it features more entryways than is typical. In addition, a small masonry wall that is no longer standing acted as a shield to the inner fire from gusts of wind once upon a time.

There are other features that make Casa Rinconada unique, though invisible to the eye. Gordon Vivian discovered that there was an antechamber beneath the floor of the Kiva and a stairwell access:

> "From one of the two antechambers on the north side of the sanctuary he found a flight of steps leading to an underground passageway which emerged in a circular structure built into the kiva's floor." (McNitt 134).

He goes on to observe that this passageway would have provided a dramatic entry for clan priests or other performers. They could enter "quite literally in the spirit of the [creation] myth-from the very bowels of the Earth." (McNitt 134).

In regards to the noticeable different between many kivas, they are easy to spot as one walks through the ruins

92

of Pueblo Bonito, Chetro Ketl, and Pueblo del Arroyo. Some of the Great Kivas have underground entrances, and some do not. An occasional rectangular kiva can be found, which predates the circular kiva, possibly as far back as the Basketmaker Era. We understand the rectangular rooms to be kivas due to the same construction beneath the ground level.

Because kivas resemble the pit-house structures of the earlier Anasazi, it is surmised that kivas evolved from the pit-house structures of the past. If this architectural evolution is true, then kivas may be structures that honor the past by being shaped in the manner of their ancestors' homes.

The construction of these massive structures was no easy feat, and again, required advanced engineering and building skill. To create a pitched roof over an open area 60'+ across requires precision and well thought out calculations. From the ground up, the planning and execution would be exacting.

"At Chetro Ketl, a structural detail associated with the four roof supports was noted later in the other Great Kivas. The lower end of each massive upright, each of which measured twenty-six inches in diameter, was set down into a circular, masonry-lined pit dug into the kiva floor. Before a post was seated, however, four enormous sandstone discs, weighing between 1000, and 1500 pounds each, had

been laid one upon another to create a solid foundation for the post." (Lister and Lister 100).

There are many different sizes of kivas at Chaco Canyon, with most of them located inside the Great Houses. The high number of kivas inspires us to believe they were used concurrently by various families, sects, clans, trade groups, and leaders, as workspaces and / or for religious ceremonies. Valuable jewelry and ritual items have been found in the ruins of kivas, and it is presumed that the kivas were also places to hide or store certain items, such as strings of beads and turquoise pendants; (Krupp 234).

Pondering the purpose and function of a kiva in Chacoan society leads one to believe that the largest ones would have been ceremonial and communal in nature. The sheer size would have accommodated upwards of 400 people at the largest kiva, Casa Rinconada. The smaller kivas present more of a puzzle, especially by their ubiquity. In modern Pueblo times, small kivas are called clan kivas, denoting their function and use is specific to a clan. Possibly, the explanation for the high number of kivas suggests a high number of families or clans.

Puebloan history suggests that kivas were controlled by the men, just as the domestic space was controlled by the women. During the 1924 excavations of Pueblo Bonito, Neil Judd revealed that the men built the kivas to the exclusion of the women, as the kivas appeared to have less craftsmanship in their overall appearance than did the other masonry in which the women were involved. By speculating that the ritual functions of the kiva have remained unchanged, it is possible that women were allowed to enter the kivas to attend important decisions and ceremonies.

In the layout of the canyon, visual lines of communication were a priority. There are small outcroppings of round mounds, unexcavated, all around the landscape. These are small house communities that have been buried by the silt of centuries of wind. Today, many of these mounds are camouflaged, covered in Russian Thistle. Nonetheless, as one stands below Casa Rinconada, it is easy to conjure up an image of it standing mighty and proud over the community of small houses along the southern shores of the Chaco Wash, taking notice of the straight road connecting Casa Rinconada to Pueblo Bonito. This ancient road would have been travelled daily and would have been a busy road, full of social exchanges. One can imagine the canyon alive with the sounds from Casa Rinconada, the dancers within, the sounds of the foot drums, and seeing and smelling the smoke of the fire that burned.

Kivas are often interpreted as direct architectural representations of spirituality, symbolic of the creation myth which is shared amongst Southwestern Tribes. This creation myth details the emergence to this world from the antechambers of the underworld. Although there are variations on this myth, there are many commonalties amongst disseminated descendants that suggest continuity of spiritual belief. Also noted—kivas are not found

95

exclusively in Chaco; they are ubiquitous in the southwest. This also lends support to the belief that kivas were a form of architecture that was constant between societies, reflecting a continuum of spiritual beliefs.

> "*A vague summation of the creation myth is that it involves a spider-woman leading the people from the underground up through an opening in the earth. This opening is known as a sipapu, or the Earth's navel. The sipapu is holy spot of emergence, coming from the darkness of the underworld to the light of this world. Now, consider the kiva as an architectural reenactment of this myth: 'Symbolically the kiva stands for a place and process of emergence. Its roof entrance is the point of emergence, and the ladder is not just a way of getting in and out, but a symbolic component of the chamber related to the myth.'*" (Krupp 233).

One can imagine the significance associated with climbing in and out of Casa Rinconada, and how it would have been a great rite of Chacoan society.

Casa Rinconada is also known as a *keyhole* kiva. This means that there is an antechamber entrance to the circular enclosure. This antechamber entrance was most likely a symbolic entrance or exit to the kiva, more closely related to the creation myth than kivas without keyhole entrances. The existence of these keyhole kivas also suggests that there must have been interaction with cultures to the north of Chaco:

"Keyhole kivas are typically found in the Mesa Verde region of Southwestern Colorado and in southeastern Utah. Their presence here indicates that ideas were exchanged between the people of Chaco and population centers to the north." (National Park Service).

This is not surprising as migration from the Mesa Verde area to Chaco is well documented in the centuries leading up to the Chaco florescence. Due to the scarcity of artifacts other than those considered sacred in this Great Kiva, ceremonial purposes were likely its sole function.

If keyhole kivas are evidence of northern influence, it is possible that the southern influence (that is known through other architectural features, such as T-shaped doors) may have clashed at Chaco, both cultures merging at Chaco Canyon. Being the middle ground, geographically and ideologically, gave an advantage where the Chacoans may have been able to capitalize economically on the competition, thereby assimilating Chacoan culture to their own.

There is evidence of additional external structures that have decayed past the point of knowing their full scale. Some reconstruction was performed on Casa Rinconada in the 1930s, more extensive reconstruction than what occurred on many other structures. The height of the walls

Kyle Widner

today is the approximation of Gordon Vivian. The summer solstice alignment may or may not have had that specific intentionality. Even without the external reconstruction, there may have been internal structural supports that obliterated the light in the niche. Furthermore, the idea that the niche was covered with a screen of plaster in order to support smaller beams above the niches indicates that there would have been a purposefully aligned sunbeam.

Anna Sofaer's research resulted in the idea that Ancient Chacoans considered alignments in cardinal directions to be sacred, and held in the mind's eye:

"The buildings at Chaco Canyon express the cosmology of its people as though to be held in the mind's eye. The major Chacoan buildings align to each other along lines to key points in the solar and lunar cycles, forming a vast celestial pattern. Many of these alignments are between buildings that are not in sight of each other. The pattern could never have been seen as a whole. It is as though the Chacoan buildings and their inter-building alignments form a harmonic unity that could be experienced only in the mind's eye…" (The Chaco Mystery).

The other Great Kivas of Chaco are ensconced *within* the Great Houses. Kin Nahasbas is also considered a free-standing Great Kiva, located about a hundred feet or so west of Una Vida, right at the base of the northern cliff. Constructed in about 1030 AD and renovated about 1100

AD. This Great Kiva is interesting in that it might be the first Great Kiva in Chaco Canyon that was used to hold ceremonial meetings for travelers, and it may have held ceremonies for more than just one community. Kin Nahasbas most distinguishing feature: it lacks wall niches.

Likely, both Kin Nahasbas and Casa Rinconada are their own free-standing units because they were meant to serve communities, rather than smaller groups such as clans or family ceremonies. Kin Nahasbas may have also served to function as a point of visual contact with other sentinel points in the canyon. Una Vida, the Great House with which Kin Nahasbas is associated, lacks visibility within the canyon, unlike Pueblo Bonito's central Great Kiva, which is almost as large as Casa Rinconada, for it measures in at about 60' in diameter. Then, right next door to Pueblo Bonito is Chetro Ketl, which has not one, but *two* Great Kivas.

> *"During Chaco's flowering in the eleventh century, a wave of religious fervor swept the canyon that was never equaled in other regions of the Southwest. A dominant factor in building activity that came at the same time…"* (McNitt 133).

Another perspective on Chacoan kivas: "The structure also became part of a suite of architectural elements representing the Chacoan worldview. The development of the Great Kiva is linked to ideas about cyclical time, social memory, directionality, and balanced dualism that were integral to an ideology legitimizing Chaco as its central place." (VanDyke 94).

Despite the reasons or motives for the kivas and Great Kivas of Chaco Canyon, one thing is certain; they all had significant roles in the daily existence of Chaco and Anasazi everywhere. With the lack of a written language, it stands to reason that kivas would have played a crucial role in the transfer of knowledge and tradition.

Ceremonies, Rituals, and Modern Practices

Chaco Canyon has been theorized to be many things; however, there is one common thread in all the interpretations of Chaco: it was a place rich with ceremony and ritual. These rituals drew in tribes and clans from great distances away. There were undoubtedly seasonal migrations to Chaco in order to view or celebrate important solstices or equinoxes.

Imagine the tribes arriving at Chaco to experience the grandeur of landscape and architecture. This was all part of the experience for these visitors of ancient times, just as it is for those who visit today. Perhaps it was even a spiritual rite to travel to Chaco, and have the privilege of retreating into a Great Kiva.

In many of the modern Puebloan and Hopi ceremonies, insight into the practices of the Anasazi in Chaco Canyon can be found. These Chacoans were exposed to the natural elements, highly dependent on the caprice of nature. In order to temper their relationship with nature, they anthropomorphized many deities, such as Tewa, the Sun God, and Spider Woman. These spirits divided into many spirits because the responsibility was too great for two to handle. In order to appease and appeal to these great spirits, Ancient Chacoans made rituals and ceremonies a part of daily existence, always wanting to show gratitude or worship in whatever way may be applicable.

Kyle Widner

It's also possible that many practices of Ancient Chacoans are practices that would be unrecognizable to the modern Puebloan, making it an anachronistic fallacy to consider the Chacoans in the context of the modern Puebloans:

> "...avoid prejudging what political structures...it is perfectly possible that forms of organization that were common prehistorically have become extinct amongst modern Pueblos..." (Sebastian 5).

Seeking plausible connections is a plausible course of action, however. Just because the modern practices, rituals, ceremonies, social structure, etc. *might not* reflect the ancient societal structure, does not preclude that they *might*. In whole or in part, as there is likelihood, which increases if one considers the Puebloan resistance to change, even today. It seems evident that spirituality played a fundamental role in Chacoan existence, despite it being challenging for the modern scholar to grasp.

> "A clear knowledge of paraphernalia and cult objects used in modern pueblo rites is a great aid to archeological work in pueblo ruins, and a familiarity with legendary history is especially helpful in identifying village sites or determining the clans that once inhabited them. Knowing the objects that survive in the cult rites of any clan a student can recognize them when found in

Kyle Widner

prehistoric ruins and thus interpret their meaning." (Fewkes, *The Butterfly*...557).

Within the kivas and Great Kivas lie the largest spiritual artifacts we have in order to decipher Chacoan spirituality. With the number of kivas out there, likely not all of them were used for rituals and ceremonies. Stephen Lekson states:

"Many archaeologists see kivas as nothing more than an activity space that happens to be in a round shape because the people who occupied them lived in round pit houses before beginning to build pueblos." (Drexler 48).

Perhaps the answers that have been sought out for so long exist within the purpose of the Great Kivas. Their sheer size suggests that many clans could have gathered under one great roof. Richard Wetherill has witnessed many modern kiva practices: not from within the kiva, but as an outsider in the community. He witnessed these kiva ceremonies in the same capacity as a Chacoan woman would have. Consider the following description of the Snake and Antelope Clan's kiva activities in the year of 1891:

Wetherill says that many women were working in the plaza, and all could hear the chants coming from different kivas. Different clans had their own kivas, and one particular kiva, the Snake Clan, had its leader emerging a few times. Wetherill took notice that everyone would respectfully ignore his presence. He describes the leader of the Snake Clan emerging from the kiva, walking through the courtyard with his face shielded by his own arm holding up his cloak of eagle feathers, all dyed red. Wetherill observed that the women and other members of the community turned their heads away. This was done in order to deferentially avoid witnessing his passage. He would walk at a fast clip to perform whatever task was at hand. No one would acknowledge him and he had an air of secrecy about his actions. He did not want to be seen, but for some putative reason, was forced to exit the kiva time again.

Wetherill's depiction gives us insight as to how those who were not part of the rituals at Pueblo Bonito would have behaved, women in particular. These ceremonies were no short affair, either, sometimes going on for days on end. Maybe they were spiritualistic for the individual, or even ritualistic for the community. We know that many of them were done in efforts to commune with nature, begging for rain.

The fact that there is such a high concentration of kivas in one place, something not noted in other areas that have been studied, plays well to the belief that ritualistic spirituality served a huge role in Ancient Chaco, with different kivas possibly being used for different rituals, depending if they were exclusive to men or inclusive of the tribe. We're thankful for Wetherill's account from an outsider's perspective, because it offers something. Since ceremonies are protected elements of Native culture, we are not privy to their intent or the ritual, itself. It was only on infrequent occasions that women were invited in to bear witness to certain ceremonies.

Many anthropologists have theorized about the relationship between myth and ceremony. Keeping in the Native character of remaining as enigmatic as possible, there are disparate theories about approaching Native mythology from the perspective that mythology and ritual are related. Apparently in Navajo culture this is the case; Navajo myths dictates their ceremonies. However, in Hopi rituals, there is not an exact relationship.

> "Ethnologists among the Hopi [as opposed to Navajo], have been little concerned with the possible existence of ties between ritual and mythology." (Titiev 31).

As a result, deciphering modern myth can sometimes mislead interpretations of the past. Still, there are also striking similarities between the Native cultures who have a homologous relationship between myth and ceremony, and those who do not, helping to reach consensus that these similarities are like studs of truth.

Another perspective to explain the multitudes of kivas in Chaco Canyon is that there needed to be a specific clan host kiva for each and every clan that came to visit

Chaco. It was critical that each clan contribute to their Chacoan kiva; possibly like an ambassador's residence. Each clan could worship at Chaco, both in their private kivas, and in the grand scale Great Kivas, which offered the ability to host many clans simultaneously. Kivas, being round, were the perfect accommodation for circle dances. Circle dances may be the oldest of ceremonial formations that are known.

> *"Circle dancing accompanied with various shaken rattles and possibly basket drums is the oldest recognizable ceremonial activity. Such dancing was a part of war rituals, puberty celebrations, or fertility ceremonies."* (Brown 374).

These ceremonies could have been grand events worthy of Mardi Gras or Carnival, including masked dancers known as "kachinas" (or an early version of kachinas). Kachinas are spirit beings, usually of ancestors. Imagine a dramatic entrance by the clan leader from the underground tunnel, which we know is thought to be analogous to the emergence myth and that it represents the sipapu—a holy navel. The dramatic flair of these ceremonies was not underplayed. They all had purpose and were possibly the social events of the tribes and clans, as well.

In a tour guide discussion with G.B. Cornucopia, he discussed a corn planting ceremony that might have gone on in Ancient Chaco. In the corn planting ceremony, he says that children and adolescents were probably woken up in the middle of the night and brought to a kiva. A woman would be standing in the middle of the circle, and she would talk to them about last year's crops and that this year should be better. She delivered a message of hope. And then, she would be surrounded by elders in the tribe and the children could hear her speaking and giving directions about how to plant for the next year. Next, a dramatic boom sounds out and—poof—a cloud of cornmeal smoke makes her disappear, because when the elders break the circle the woman is gone. All that is left is a basket of corn. Her voice is still heard as though she is a spirit of the corn; (Cornucopia CVB). Cornucopia says that playing out such a ceremony causes a more vivid realization. Just imagining it as you read it in these pages tends to bring it to life.

Not surprisingly, there is also disagreement about the nature of kiva ceremonies. There are some scholars who do not believe that the ceremonies that are practiced today necessarily shed any light on the past:

> *"I do not believe that the Chacoans held their rituals in hundreds upon hundreds of small, dark, smoky, and dangerous pits. Rather, evidence is continuing to emerge that they held their ceremonies on platform mounds and perhaps even pyramids, as did all highly organized Native American cultures during that time period."* (Fisher).

Fisher's theory seems to indicate that they may have treated the trash middens located in front of the Great Houses as ceremonial mounds.

It seems that out of the entire Chaco puzzle, there is only one point of agreement, one similarity between disparities: the idea that Chaco was an epicenter for cultural rituals and ceremonies is probable, as it explains the roads, outside influences that are evident in food sources and items such as turquoise, and the vast number of dwellings.

What we know for certain is that Chaco was a cultural complex, likely an epicenter for cultural exchange, and that the Great Kivas play a great part. Ceremonies and rituals would have been the lifeblood of the Chacoan culture, as evidenced in the ritualistically motivated architecture and numerous ceremonial artifacts.

**This book is property of
Lee VerMulm's
personal library**

Roads

Hundreds of miles of roads spoke outwards from Chaco proper, their purpose and utility unknown. What would be the need for an elaborate road system, aligned in cardinal directions, with roads uniformly 30' wide, excavated down to bedrock, most of which lead to no obvious destination? It is possible that they led *somewhere*, at some point, but the modern locations are lost to time and the elements, or unknowable to modern interpretation. "These guys could get around just fine without 30 foot-wide roads cutting straight across the landscape," says archaeologist John Stein of the Navajo Nation, a leading scholar on the subject:

> *"A three-foot-wide path would have been room enough for a tradesman backpacking pots from Chaco to one of the distant outliers. No draft animals or wheeled carts used them, no armies marched on them; they were over engineered and underused. They must have served some other purpose."* (Wicklein 37).

These are not simple roads or paths. They represent incredible effort in excavation and construction. There would be no other way to end up with such a precise road—30' wide, and built without regard to topography or natural obstacle.

One other puzzling characteristic of Chaco roads is the appearance of parallel road segments, identified at both the North Road and South Road.

An extreme example is on the North Road, above Pierre's Ruin. Here, 4 segments, each spaced less than 40 meters apart, appear to be almost perfectly parallel, via a bird's eye view. Such redundancy seems to suggest a ceremonial or ritual purpose for the roads, as no obvious functional purpose appears logical.

Stairways on the canyon walls were sculpted to allow access from the floor of the canyon to the roads on the mesa above. Logically, the roads would connect Chaco proper to outlying Chacoan communities, but the roads were built after the outlying communities already existed.

Estimates vary as to the extent of the road system, ranging from 150–400 total miles of connected roads and as previously mentioned, one cannot help but notice how arrow-straight they are, not yielding to natural topographical obstacles. The builders did not deter their route according to actual topography. To do this, the builders removed earth and vegetation, using those excavated materials to build berms. The feat becomes further impressive by taking note of the extensive road cuts that were made where the road crosses land elevations.

"Another extraordinary feature is their striking linearity and their 'dog-legged'

Kyle Widner

turns. Chacoan roads are laid out along straight lines. A road continues its bearing for miles. When it turns, it does so with a sudden angular, jog. Then the new course continues until the next dog-legged turn." (Frazier 107).

The only way that modern scientists can still see the roads is from the depressions they created. Moisture accumulates a bit faster in the depth of these depressions, and this causes the vegetation that grows on these roads to have a different color than the surrounding vegetation. Additionally, these depressions are consistently 20'-30' wide, and they are demarcated by the eye because of the berms of broken substrate to make the road, which is piled strategically to the sides. They made staircases, ramps and even causeways. This means they actually elevated the road surface above the ground-level:

"In places they constructed causeways, places where both sides of the road bend have been raised above the surrounding terrain. One such causeway is near Peñasco Blanco…" (Frazier 108).

The Chacoans did not simply erect the causeways, but they employed some of their masonry techniques to its construction as well.

"The Chacoans put in fill to raise the road bend in two long areas. One of the areas has

111

masonry borders two feet high and twelve feet long." (Frazier 108).

The roads adhere to the cardinal directions with little deviation. The north / south meridian is expressed in the North Road and the South Road. These roads are more pronounced and developed than the other roads. When factoring in the repetition of this cardinal direction, such as in the central wall of Pueblo Bonito's plaza, it is clear the north / south direction was important to the Anasazi.

Additionally, if one considers the creation myths, when it is identified, it is typically north and south. There is significant agreement in these migrations myths amongst modern descendants. By following the lengthy roads that extend from downtown Chaco, climbing resolutely over cliff faces, crossing barren mesas, and plunging through canyons, it is tempting to generalize that *all roads lead to Chaco.* But it may be that all roads lead *away* from Chaco to other sacred sites.

Lekson argues that these roads were a form of architecture and *not* part of an infrastructure; that the Great North Road is definitely a road from Chaco to the Aztec outlier via the Salmon Ruins outlier; (The Chaco Meridian 131). An additional argument that Lekson makes is that the Great North Road facilitated a connection to an emerging community rather than the idea that the communities and outliers all pre-dated the construction of the roads:

Kyle Widner

"The North Road, far more difficult to date than the buildings it connects-may have been built in the late 1080s and the early 1100's...that is during the planning and initial construction at Salmon and Aztec. If so the road did not connect two existing places; it connected an old place with a new place, an emerging place." (The Chaco Meridian 131).

Also in *The Chaco Meridian*, Lekson speculates:

"Chacoan roads are enigmatic: no wheeled vehicles, no beasts of burden, no bulk transport other than porters. Why a road? <u>Porters walk in line, single file.</u>" (The Chaco Meridian 130).

One problem with the utilitarian interpretation of the road system is that there really was not much of a "system".

"Considered from a utilitarian perspective, however, the road appears to be overbuilt and underused...Important features of the road - its extraordinary width and the redundancy of its routes - have no satisfactory functional explanation. The road averages 30 feet in width - wider than a modern two-lane road and far wider than any of the other prehistoric roads or trails of

the Southwest outside of the Chaco cultural region. The width is greater than required for draft animals or wheeled vehicles. Since this culture had neither, the width seems especially excessive in practical terms." (The Great North Road).

"Whatever the case, the Anasazi 'roads' required extensive human labor. Why would the Anasazi invest so much human energy into these public works projects, when there was no tradition for building roads and none of their neighbors built roads?" (The Anasazi Road System).

The parallel roads are evidence that the roads may have been firstly a cosmological expression, before being a usable route. Therefore, like the architecture and mass of the construction of the Great Houses, the roads are similar in their grandeur, lack of utility, and strict adherence to the sacred meridian. Their purpose was not for traveling to a destination, as much as the road, itself, may have been the destination.

In "The Mystery of Chaco Canyon", a modern Puebloan explains the act of intentionally breaking pottery vessels rendered them unusable for the physical world; once broken, it is released to the spirit world, ready for use. If roads were ceremonial, as pottery occasionally was, perhaps no utilitarian purpose was intended. Pottery could be both functional and ceremonial, so why not the roads?

"A recent inventory of the Great North Road has produced no evidence that indicates extensive use for the transportation of economic goods... The absence of hearths and ground or chipped stone in the road inventory suggests there was little encampment along the road." (The Great North Road).

Some modern Puebloans see the North Road as leading to the *sipapu*, which may be (physically or metaphorically) located in Kutz Canyon. The sipapu symbolizes the portal through which ancient ancestors first emerged into the present world. Many Native Americans creation legends share elements of the sipapu story. In keeping with the theme of the emergence myth and its similarities as seen in the construction and lay-out of the North Road, it is important to note that Kutz Canyon is considered sacred to many modern descendants of the Anasazi. These modern descendants believe that Kutz Canyon is the actual place of emergence. After the clans emerged, they had to migrate because the sipapu was a holy place, not a communal place. It is important for each clan to revisit the sipapu in order to remember their spiritual path. Also, it is thought that the ancient spirits and the spirits of the yet-born travel these routes. In this manner, by making these paths into a spiritual ritual of travel, the Anasazi could come into contact with their elders who had passed, and communicate with future generations. Because of this, it is entirely possible that the Great North Road led

115

Kyle Widner

to where Ancient Anasazi believed that the emergence myth took place.

A description of the Great North Road given by Anna Sofaer of The Solstice Project:

The Great North Road has its origin in several routes, which ascend by staircases carved into the cliff from Pueblo Bonito and Chetro Ketl in Chaco Canyon, which are the two largest structures of the Chaco region. These routes converge at Pueblo Alto, a large structure located close to the north rim of the canyon. From there the road runs 13 degrees to the east of north for 3 km to Escavada Wash. It then heads within 1/2 percent of true north for 16km, where it articulates with Pierre's Complex, an unusual cluster of small buildings on knobs and pinnacles. The road then heads close to 2 degrees east of north for 31 km and ends at Kutz Canyon. It appears to terminate at three small, isolated sites, and a stairway recently located by the Solstice Project that descends from the Kutz Canyon escarpment to the canyon floor.

Possibly, there were ceremonial pilgrimages on these roads during important equinox or solstice occasions. These pilgrimages may have been a reenactment of the emergence myth, or may have been a way to connect the past, present, and future. One theorist, John Wicklein, portrays a possible version of what could have been a ceremonial recurrent ritual for the Anasazi:

"Anasazi pilgrims gathered on the floor of Kutz Canyon in northwestern New Mexico, at a point on the south wall just below Upper Twin Angels Mound - the place of the sipapu, where their ancestors had first emerged from the underworld. Led in procession by their sun priest, they ascended a large wooden stairway that climbed the canyon wall. On the rim, they paused to place offerings at several small shrines. Then they began a journey down a road, uniformly 30 feet wide, which led straight south for 31 miles to Pueblo Bonito, the Great House at Chaco Canyon that the Anasazi knew as Middle Place, the center of their spiritual world. They believed the spirits of the newborn also traveled this path, as did those of the dead when they returned to the underworld through the sipapu. Just as their ancestors had done when they first emerged from the underworld, the pilgrims separated into clan groups halfway to Middle Place and followed four parallel roads for about a mile, then rejoined as one group on a single road." (Wicklein 37).

117

Kyle Widner

The South Road could also support the emergence myth, as the North Road is thought to connect to the sipapu, the navel to the underground, the South Road is thought to terminate with of the tallest geographical features on the landscape, Hosta Butte.

> *"The South Road, on the other hand, leads to a shrine on a prominent butte. Marshall believes this pinnacle was the southern pole of a Chacoan axis mundi, that the pathway up the butte was a ceremonial way to the heavens, in contrast to the descent to the underworld at the sipapu where the North Road ends."* (Wicklein 39).

Therefore, if the North Road directs the spirit to the sipapu, back to the center of the earth, then the South Road directs the spirit upward toward the heavens.

> *"The South Road is not the only road which leads to Hosta Butte. The repetition of routes to Hosta Butte may also have been a recreation of the native mythology. However, at least three road segments do appear to be directed towards Hosta Butte...Hosta Butte is an important feature of cosmography of indigenous groups...many shrines and offerings have been found on top."* (Kanter, "Ancient Roads" 57).

Kyle Widner

The roads were only discovered with the advent of aerial cartography, as they are nearly indecipherable on foot. However, by air, the 30' wide depressions are quite evident.

"Since each type of vegetation or soil emits a different amount of heat, and the differences can be detected by thermal sensors, they can be plotted into a composite that reveals the outline of a road." (Wicklein 39).

Or in Anna Sofaer's words:

"To summarize, the road's great width and parallel routes, its ephemeral practical use, and apparent terminus at an isolated badlands canyon fail to justify, in functional terms, the effort entailed in its construction. The road apparently goes 'nowhere' and displays a level of effort far out of proportion to the meager tangible benefits that may have been realized from it. In many important respects, the road appears to be its own reason for development—an end in itself." (The Great North Road).

Ancient Rome was supported by a massive road network that enabled rapid support to any part of the Roman Empire, thus the saying, "all roads lead to Rome". But Chacoan roads leave us no such satisfaction, as they are yet another puzzle piece that has no obvious fit.

Outliers

There are 252 outlier buildings or structures identified in the Chaco Archive Database. Chacoan outliers are defined as pre-historic buildings or groups of buildings in the San Juan River Basin that share traits with sites in Chaco Canyon proper. Proper identification is very crude in some cases; assumptions are made simply by the size of the rubble pile. Many of these ruins are in very poor condition, with fallen walls. Most have not been excavated, making accurate tree-ring dating difficult. A majority of the dating estimates are based on types of pottery found around the sites. This compounds the problem of trying to establish the spread of the Chacoan sphere, and creates a bit of a chicken and egg quandary.

Did Chaco proper spring up as a center of trade or storage, supporting the outlier communities?

Or did Chaco wield so much influence, the outlying communities sprouted to be close the "Capital"?

Some theorize small house site communities tried to emulate buildings and kivas they had seen in Chaco, to mimic the power and standing of the Great Houses in the canyon proper.

Others speculate Chacoans created farmhouses and trading centers outside of the canyon to grow more food, or trade more goods. These outliers could have helped balance

Kyle Widner

out seasonal advantages / disadvantages, such as lack of water for growing corn. One piece of architectural evidence that backs up this notion of food supply is that the Great Houses appear to be made primarily for food storage. Many of the rooms have no evidence of human inhabitation, nor do the rooms offer the necessary ventilation for inhabitation. These rooms appear to be inaccessible storage units, dark and hard to access, ideal for storage, protected from the sun, and protected from rodents.

> *"Spreading the horticultural endeavors over the Chaco Plateau and controlling the dispersal of goods not immediately needed would have tended to balance out the vagaries of nature typical the region."* (Lister and Lister 170).

Another explanation for these outlying communities is that they were a safety net for downtown Chaco. If we take the most distant outlier community, identified as Chimney Rock, we find several points of interest to support this. It is thought that Chimney Rock could have been used to send smoke or fire signals to Huerfano Peak, and then from Huerfano Peak to Fajada Butte, which is in the canyon proper. It would take a clear day, but tests have shown it is possible.

Only 20% of this single Great House at Chimney Rock has been excavated, but it appears to have trait similarities. The main structure was a multistoried building with 55 ground level rooms and about 20 second story rooms. There are also 2 kivas, built in the Chacoan style of core and veneer masonry, which did not exist prior to Chaco. Besides serving as a signal post, there is evidence of astronomical tracking, particularly lunar standstills, which occur in an 18.6 year cycle. To add to the mystique, it also appears that Chimney Rock could have been a logging station, an encampment for workers harvesting the large ponderosa pines used to build the Chaco Canyon Great Houses.

Salmon Ruin is another prominent outlying community, found between Chaco (45 miles to the south) and Mesa Verde (45 miles to the north), in the heart of the middle San Juan Region. The main building had about 150 ground floor rooms, and 100 second story rooms. There are only 2 Chaco era kivas, a Great Kiva in the plaza, and a rare elevated kiva in the central room block. Tree-ring data suggests a very compressed building span of only 12 years, 1088-1100, and that it was only occupied for a brief period of time, being abandoned in 1130.

Based on dating estimates of pottery found at Salmon Ruin, it was likely reoccupied by Mesa Verde immigrants from 1180-1240, but by the time the general abandonment of the Colorado Plateau in 1300 occurred, Salmon Ruin was already lying empty and still. These outlying communities, Great Houses, Great Kivas, and small house sites with which the Anasazi culture is most often associated offer evidence of the influence of the Chacoan system throughout a remarkably wide area. It drew people back then, just as it draws people today.

Fajada Gap, Fajada Butte, and The Sun Dagger

Driving into Chaco Canyon from either access route, the traveler encounters unexpectedly primitive dirt roads, serving as a soft barrier against invasion by the faint of heart. Once penetrating this soft membrane against the drive-by tourist, the first reward is Fajada Butte.

This prominent landmark juts 443' from the canyon floor, splitting the middle of the Fajada Gap, a wide break in the monolith Chacra Mesa. The butte is a remnant piece of the long eroded mesa, a snapshot of time in eons of wind, water, sun, and what remains resembles a watercolor of the gods. Elegant and regal from all angles, it remains an otherworldly sentinel hovering over the east entry of the canyon.

Fajada translates from Spanish as "belted" or "banded", deriving its name from layers of exposed dark shale and low-grade coal wrapping its circumference.

The first mention of Fajada Gap and Fajada Butte in recorded history was by Jose Antonio Vizcarra, a Mexican soldier who also served as Governor of New Mexico from 1822-1823. While he was conducting an expedition against the Navajos in 1823, he came across Chaco Canyon, making a record of its ruins. He noted this remarkable formation in his 1823 journal, calling it "Cerrito Fajado". Later, US Army Lieutenant James Simpson and his guide

Carravahal discovered Chaco Canyon on an expedition, exploring its 8 large ruins. It was Carravahal who gave the Spanish names to buildings in the area, including Pueblo Bonito.

Fajada Butte: The Sun Dagger site is on the top of this 135 meter butte, capable of tracking the solstices, equinoxes, and the 18.6 year lunar standstill cycle.

The closest Chacoan structure to the gap is Una Vida, one of the three earliest Great Houses. This site offers the easiest access to the canyon, therefore it is likely that it was also a place where the Anasazi would have stood guard, watching over the canyon and alerting the locals to approaching visitors.

A survey of the terrain around the butte reveals it could be very fertile due to the drainage of Chaco Wash through the area. This potential agricultural concentration may also be the reason for clusters of small house sites in the area. This also lends credibility that the Chacoan South Road may have had a connection or terminus in Fajada Gap, extending perhaps to Una Vida. But, perhaps, most intriguing of all, the butte *is a natural site for astronomical observations, with its clear views to distant horizons.*"(Sofaer, A Unique S).

Fajada Butte plays host to what may be the most interesting site in all of southwest pre-history—The Sun Dagger. Artist Anna Sofaer was documenting rock art in 1977 when she noticed two petroglyphs pecked into the rock face behind three huge slabs of sandstone, leaning against the upper cliff face. What caught her eye was the play of light across the petroglyph. Intrigued, she returned on the day of the summer solstice to confirm her belief that this was an ancient astronomical mechanism. It was.

The slices of space between the slabs create a play of light and shadow across the petroglyphs, depending on the location of the sun during the course of the year. At the peak of the sun on the day of the summer solstice, a thin triangular shaft of light penetrates the exact middle of the larger petroglyph, signifying the summer solstice. She called this "The Sun Dagger". Over the years, this mechanism proved to be much more sophisticated than first realized. Not only did it mark the arrival of solstices and equinoxes, it also accuracy tracks an 18.6 year cycle of the moon, marking its major and minor standstills. Could this have been the main calendar of the Chacoan civilization?

From this discovery, The Solstice Project was born, resulting in further fascinating and important revelations about the astronomy of Chaco Canyon. They also produced a highly recommended documentary, "The Mystery of Chaco Canyon", narrated by Robert Redford.

> *"We found the relationship between the shapes and the resultant light patterns on the cliff is a complex one and required a sophisticated appreciation of astronomy and geometry for its realization."* (Sofaer, Chaco Astronomy 23).

The Solstice Project dates the construction of The Sun Dagger as being within the Chaco Golden Age of 950-1150 AD. Incredibly, modern observers were only given a brief, 12year window to study the site of The Sun Dagger. In 1989, it was discovered that the massive sandstone slabs generating the display had shifted slightly, forever destroying the shadowplay of light that created the most sophisticated pre-historic calendar known.

Any discussion regarding the construction and purpose of the Chacoan Great Houses always includes reference to their strict adherence to north / south / east / west orientation. This leads one to believe that the sun and moon, along with cardinal directions they dictate, were of critical importance to the Chacoan architects. The intentional alignment of walls in the Great Houses, most notably the north / south wall in Pueblo Bonito, is a major clue. The next step is to conclude strong connections

Kyle Widner

existed between the architecture of these monuments and the relevant societal structure, i.e. the belief system that conceived and created them. There is little doubt Chacoan society was deeply rooted in cosmological awareness and expression. Was this awareness tied primarily to spiritual aspects of belief, or more practical considerations like when to plant or harvest?

Further evidence lies in the solar and lunar alignments within the Great Kivas, the grand scale roads, and the intentional alignments of the buildings with other buildings.

In summary, there is a strong case for Anasazi astronomy as the overriding factor in the design, location, and development of the Great House structures of Chaco Canyon and outlying communities. Anasazi engineers and architects executed a complex and intricate series of building projects, with sustained progress over several generations, without the use of written language, all closely aligned with a connection to the solar and lunar cycles.

127

Burials

In archaeology, burials are a crucial source of information about a society, how people lived, how they died, and what was valued. A burial marks a precise point in time, providing rich and detailed data about the deceased, as well as those who cared for and buried the body. Information is gleaned about daily life, customs, rituals, and beliefs. Burials signify more than just a means of disposing of dead bodies; they are culturally influenced rituals, designed to either show respect, or in some cases, intentional disrespect, for the deceased.

The study of the graveyard at Chaco should be rich with information and insight about the lives, customs, and rituals of its citizens…if there was a graveyard. And if you are following the general theme of this book, you're not going to be surprised to hear that there is no graveyard; at least not one that has ever been found. What does this leave us with? The fact that we know of 12 generations of people living and working in Chaco Canyon, and only about 300 burials have ever been found.

Two obvious solutions come to mind. First, there is a mass burial site yet to be excavated; but this is unlikely due to sophisticated aerial thermal cartographic techniques available, which have been used in this area. Secondly, the bodies were cremated. This is also unlikely, as there are no indications of cremation chambers, burned spots, or pieces of charred bones anywhere.

"Besides…cremation was rarely, if ever, practiced by the Anasazi…" (Frazier 162).

Fairly recently, in 1974, the Chaco Center re-checked the theory of cremation. Previously, 6 large sunken masonry boxes had been discovered, but not checked for the presence of human remains or cremation. The interiors of these boxes were scorched, so it was evident that they had contained fires. However, there was no evidence of cremation in the re-excavation; (Frazier 162).

One final mark against the cremation theory concerns the wood required for the process. Rare in the canyon, and difficult to import, wood for fire was a valuable resource, and it is unlikely they would use it for cremation when other methods of disposing of the dead were available.

So the question remains unanswered: what happened to the dead? Neil Judd believed that the inability to find Pueblo Bonito's cemetery added to the Chaco mystery:

> *"With an estimated peak population of over 1,000, and with one section inhabited perhaps 250 years, Pueblo Bonito should have experienced between 4,700 and 5,400 deaths. How the bodies were disposed of and where, continue to be tantalizing puzzles."* (Frazier 160).

129

It is highly unlikely that we will ever know more than we do now. Within the *Native American Antiquities Act* and the *Native American Grave Protection Act*, there are precise, strict laws, which prohibit the search for, exhumation, or examination of ancient burials without the consent of descendants. These laws are written and enforced to protect and honor the spiritual beliefs of modern descendants.

From the burials that have been found and studied, there is evidence that 2 classes of people lived simultaneously in the canyon. They may or may not have been separate cultures or races, but the difference in average heights lends credence to this theory. These two classes interacted, but there are significant differences in how they handled their dead. At the Great House sites, the dead are carefully entombed and adorned with jewels. In the small house sites, the dead are put in a trash heap and often covered with a stone slab. These differences in burials helps to confirm what the architecture of Chaco Canyon suggests: a hierarchy of some sort existed. There were elite and non-elite Chacoans.

As to the burials "put in a trash heap", this is technically correct, but may lack context. "Middens" are large piles of refuse typically found in front of Anasazi ruins. But what we moderns see as a trash heap may have been practiced more as a ceremonial exercise. We know that intentionally broken pots are said to be released from "this world" and upon being smashed and made unusable, are then available to be used in the "next world". In this context, placing the body of a family member in a midden, when viewed as a ceremonial platform, along with broken goods, may be seen as a portal to send the person onto the next world.

The most famous and intriguing burial excavation at Chaco Canyon is known as Room 33. This is one of the smallest and earliest built rooms in the Pueblo Bonito Great House, and fairly centralized within Pueblo Bonito, essentially making it the heart of the Great House, and by extension, the heart of Chaco.

"Room 33 held the remains of at least 14 individuals and the richest assemblage of artifacts ever uncovered in the Pueblo Southwest, although it is one of the smallest rooms in the pueblo with dimension of 2 × 2 meters." (Plog and Heitman).

Entombed in this room was "Skeleton 14", an enigmatic figure I've dubbed "The Turquoise Priest". George Pepper and Richard Wetherill performed the excavation of Room 33 during the Hyde Expedition. Pepper published this account of the excavation, and discovery of Room 33's most decorated burial:

"The next skeleton found (No. 14) was in situ. The head was in an upright position, and was 7 ft. 9 in. from the ceiling-beams. The face was turned toward the southeast, and the lower jaw was in place. The upper

jaw was broken, and had fallen apart. The right side of the cranium was crushed, and there were two holes and a gash in the frontal bone. The skeleton, which was intact, was extended about north and south. The arms extended along the sides of the body. The legs were bent upward, the feet being close together, and resting against the southern wall. In view of the fact that the objects found with this body were in place, they will be considered before a general résumé of the specimens found with the other bodies is given. The skeleton itself was resting on a layer of wood-ashes which had been spread on the leveled floor of yellow sand. From the general care bestowed on this body, and from the character and quantity of the objects found with it, the deceased must have been a person of rank.' (Pepper "Pueblo Bonito").

This skeleton, The Turquoise Priest, was evidently buried with care and unimaginable riches for the time. The fact that the right side of the cranium was crushed, with two holes and a gash signifies he did not die a peaceful death, perhaps providing evidence of a social upheaval. Why would someone be killed so violently, then buried so reverently? Unless one of the lower class members, in a fit of violent anger, took matters into his own hands and killed the upper-class leader. The upper class, horrified, gave The Turquoise Priest burial with high honors.

In addition, according to R. Gwinn Vivian, The Turquoise Priest was nearly 6' tall, which meant he would have towered over the average Chacoan. It is thought that The Turquoise Priest may have been 45-50 years old, as well, which is remarkable for the time.

Judd continues to describe the ornate burial in detail, numbering the turquoise beads at well over 10,000. No other burial like this has been found in the entire Anasazi range. Turquoise beads adorned his chest, multiple strands of necklaces; he had bracelets made of turquoise, and pendants of jet and turquoise. These findings are staggering, considering that 80% of all the turquoise ever found in Chaco Canyon was found in Room 33:

> *"Associated with those burials in Room 33 were tens of thousands of turquoise beads and pendants that comprise a large portion of all of the turquoise jewelry ever recovered from the canyon—constituting more than 80% of all turquoise found in Chaco—as well as large quantities of shell and jet and highly unusual artifacts such as flutes, wooden ceremonial staffs, cylinder jars, and conch shell trumpets."* (Plog and Heitman).

But the riches don't stop with turquoise, as there were 9 wooden flutes excavated from Room 33, along with many other unique artifacts:

"Equally noteworthy are many unusual items such as two cylinder jars, almost two dozen wooden ceremonial sticks, a shell trumpet, two cylindrical baskets covered with turquoise and shell mosaic, and nine flutes. The wooden flutes are the only ones ever recovered from Chaco Canyon and are rare throughout the northern American Southwest." (Plog and Heitman).

Room 33 also included the burial of 12 women, arranged around The Turquoise Priest, each with a hole in their cranium, as well. Were they also murdered? Or sacrificed to accompany The Turquoise Priest into the afterlife? The findings in this room give pause to those who prefer viewing Chaco as a peaceful, utopian, egalitarian society. Were these violent deaths simply a crime, the "Helter Skelter" of the day, or evidence of a subjugated underclass rising up in revolt?

The Turquoise Priest is one of the oldest burials in Pueblo Bonito, probably interred about 875 AD. This would be about 25 years after the first stones were laid out to build Pueblo Bonito. Above his burial, it is conjectured by Pepper that Skeleton 13 may have been buried at the same time as The Turquoise Priest. There is a barrier of intentionally placed sand between Skeletons' 13 and 14; then above Skeleton 13 is a wooden planked floor. The other 12 skeletons were placed above the planks, buried with not more than a light dusting of dirt.

The excavated burials of the surrounding small houses versus those at the Great Houses reveal that there *is* medical evidence that these people buried in the Great Houses were elite, beyond the highly decorated and ornate burials. Scientific analysis reveals the individuals buried at the Great Houses enjoyed a healthier diet than commoners, who dwelt and were buried around the small house structures. And they were taller than those who lived as commoners. The evidence of better diets is determined through anemic iron deficient bones found in the excavated burials of the small houses; (Judd, *The Architecture of Chaco Canyon* 140). The nitrogen isotopes found in the Great House burials also indicate a diet that was high in protein.

Some theorize that Chaco was only seasonally inhabited. This might explain the dearth of burials; if the population migrated, then maybe only healthy people made the trip into Chaco, and the elders, or the sick would die elsewhere. This theory makes sense given the harshness of winter in Chaco. Tom Windes' hearth analysis would thereby become an inadequate measure of population; if the majority of the population were not in the houses during winter, then there would not be a need for many fire hearths.

The only conclusive evidence that burials have provided is that there was some sort of difference in quality of lifestyle for those who were buried ceremoniously. These burials of the Great Houses are clearly of a different

135

Kyle Widner

quality than those of the small house communities. R. Gwinn Vivian's theorized 2 separate cultures, with separate ideologies coexisted in Chaco Canyon. If his theory is correct, it could explain the disparity between the types of burials and the physical differences between them. Having noted that The Turquoise King seems to have been 45–50 years old, it is staggering to consider that 45% of children under age 5 died. That is nearly half the population, gone before their fifth year of life. It is estimated that the average Chacoan woman had 4 births and died during their child-bearing years, never experiencing menopause. If a child made it to age 15, then the life expectancy would reliably be another 19 years; (Stuart and McKinsey 157). With these mortality figures, it is truly inexplicable where all the deceased disappeared to. Additionally, at the Great Houses, there was minimal evidence of burials within the middens, which contrasts with this being more common in the small houses.

As a result of the noted facts and evidence, some scholars now conclude that few people lived in the Great Houses, suggesting their primary purpose was more ritualistic, ceremonial, or serving as storage, versus residences.

The Navajos discovered and looted Chaco before the arrival of Simpson, Judd, and Wetherill. Judd noted that in 1920, none of the middens were left undisturbed; all had been looted; (Plog and Heitman). The Wetherills journaled that they were certain there was a great deal of early pot hunting, and therefore, also the destruction of burial sites;

(Frazier 164). This sadly means that there were likely many intact burial sites lost forever due to looters seeking turquoise and other valuable items.

Like most other questions regarding Chaco, the disconnect between the number of people who would have worked, lived, and played in Chaco Canyon and the number of burials located contributes to the mystery.

Volcanoes and Skywatchers

In 1958, dendrochronologist Terah Smiley studied tree-ring data from several beams of the 100 room Wupatki Pueblo, located 15 miles northeast of Sunset Crater, near Flagstaff, Arizona. The purpose was to determine the year and duration of a massive eruption, and concluded it occurred during the winter of 1064-1065 AD. As a result, a date of 1064 AD for the Sunset Crater eruption became accepted in both the geological and archaeological record. Later studies using a variety of chemical assays and detailed tree-ring morphology indicate that this date is likely inaccurate. Evidence now suggests that Sunset Crater most likely erupted in the mid-to-late 1080s AD.

Why is this significant to Chaco? The Sunset Crater eruption site is only 200 miles from Chaco as the raven flies. A dramatic cloud of ash and darkened skies would have had serious consequences on the growing season, shortening it with colder temperatures. This would have a negative effect on the wellbeing of the Chacoans and their psyche, as well. By moving the date of the eruption to the mid-1080s, the drama continues as this segues into the worst drought of the 11th century, with remarkably dry summers in the 1090s. How did the Chacoans respond? Around 1100, they started construction on 5 massive structures: Casa Chaquita, New Alto, Kin Kletso, Wijiji, and Tsin Kletzin. Were they trying to appease the gods with new construction honoring the great spirits? If they were, perhaps it worked, from 1100-1130 both the summer rains and annual rainfall were well in excess of long term

138

averages, and the 5 new buildings were completed during this time. Three of the new buildings were slightly different; they were built with the "McElmo Phase" style of masonry, which had open plazas, versus the previously seen Chacoan style, with subdivided rooms, arc-shaped barriers, and enclosed plazas. What drove these changes, and were the changes related to the environmental phenomenon of the times? Again, it's unknown, leaving us to draw intelligent conclusions based off of what we do know.

One of the striking features of Chaco is the dominating sky. With few trees or other impediments to the view, the sky feels omnipresent. When you combine the lack of horizon while actually in the canyon proper, and the high cliff walls, there is a "cocoon" sensation. Each edge of the canyon you see, even through the Fajada or South Gaps, looks like the edge of the world. At night, the lack of surrounding light pollution leads to spectacular stargazing. Planets and stars pierce the night sky like diamond needles. The rising of the moon is dramatic and arrives on stage like a movie star making a grand entrance.

Perhaps even more than ancient peoples elsewhere, Chacoans strove to be at one with the natural cycles of Father Sky and Mother Earth. Tracking the seasons was not just ceremony and theater; planting or harvesting at the wrong time would mean the difference between a surplus and possible starvation. In the Zuni language, the word for life is the same as daylight: *tekohanane*.

Kyle Widner

For a culture that lived at the mercy of the rains and natural forces around them, being able to track and anticipate the sun and moon cycles must have provided a much needed sense of control or connection. As the days leading into winter grew shorter, with the noon sun lower, a sense of dread may have descended upon the people, as they perhaps did not know for certain that the cycle would reverse. There must have been relief each year after the winter solstice, when the sun would slowly rise earlier in the day and reach higher into the sky. Ceremonies, festivals, and feasts would certainly celebrate these major annual milestones—going from the depths of winter to a tepid first step back to spring and into the full blossom of summer. Sun Priests would bear the responsibility of erecting tracking stations, monitoring the results, and making pronouncements that all would be anticipating. They held an important, prominent role in the community.

This responsibility did not stop with the decline of Chaco, it has continued with some of the Pueblo descendants, including the Hopi. Don Talayesva, a Hopi Indian born in 1890 wrote an autobiographic book called "Sun Chief". He wrote:

"The point of sunrise on the shortest day of the year was called the sun's winter home and point of sunrise on the longest day its summer home. Old Talasemptewa, who was almost blind, would sit out on the housetop of the special Sun Clan house and watch the sun's progress toward its summer home. He

untied a knot in a string for each day. When the sun arose at certain mesa peaks, he passed the word around that it was time to plant sweet corn, ordinary corn, string beans, melons squash, lima beans and other seeds. On a certain date, he would announce that it was too late for any more planting."

The Zuni Indians have similar rituals, whereby the Sun Priest and Master Priest seat themselves in a specific place and watch the play of the sun and shadow. Notches are made in a calendar made of pinewood. This calendar would guide the labor schedules, religious ceremonies, even recreational and leisure activities.

Notice the similarities between these two Anasazi descendant tribes, as they track the seasons by following the position of the sun against known markers. By extrapolating backwards, we can easily imagine similar processes in the Anasazi world.

The most isolated and easternmost Chacoan ruin is Wijiji. Nearby, on the upper reaches of the canyon wall, rests a white-painted symbol strikingly similar to symbols found at the Zuni sun-watching station. The symbols feature rays pointing outwards in four directions. From a spot on the ledge near the apparent sun symbol of Wijiji, the winter solstice sunrise emerges from behind the top of a pillar, a clear expression of the sun's southernmost point in the sky. Another possible Chacoan sky watching station may be the unusual corner windows in Pueblo Bonito. Two

Kyle Widner

of them face the southeast, and the one in Room 228 could have been used to observe the arrival of the solstice.

The Great Kiva Casa Rinconada could have contained multiple solar and lunar marking mechanisms, with its upper portion extending above ground level, unusual for Chaco kivas. There are two rows of equally spaced, rectangular niches around the interior. East of the northern entrance to the kiva is a small window that permits light to enter. One niche is dramatically, and near-perfectly illuminated on the morning of the summer solstice, about a half hour after sunrise. This may be coincidence, we can never know for sure. Despite all of this, a major problem with any interpretation of Casa Rinconada is the massive restoration projects that have been undertaken, which means that the stones may not be in the same positions that they were during Chacoan times.

With volcanoes as an example, the forces of nature can be uncontrolled and possibly devastating to a civilization so closely tied to the earth as the Chacoans were. The predictability of the sun and moon, combined with the residents' ability to closely track the cycles and seasons that followed, may have given the people a sense of control that they would have struggled to attain in other parts of their lives.

Supernovas and Strange Skies

During the Chaco phenomenon, there have been several strange astronomical events documented. We can never know how they were interpreted, what changes they may have caused in society, or if they were viewed with awe and appreciation or abject fear. However, for people so connected with the cycles of sun and moon, we are certain they would not have been ignored. The interpretation, though, is something that will always be a curiosity that can never be satisfied.

Here is the chronology of the known strange astronomical events that would have been seen by the Chacoans:

- History records that on December 22, 968 there was a total solar eclipse near the winter solstice.
- Halley's Comet made an appearance in 989, and then again in 1066.
- On April 30, 1006, the brightest supernova in recorded history appeared. This star remained low on the southern horizon for almost 3 months. It was bright enough to cast a shadow from its light.
- Finally, the most well-documented supernova appeared on July 4, 1054, likely documented in Chaco as the supernova pictograph below Peñasco Blanco.

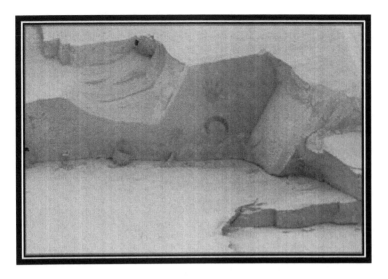

Pictograph of supernova that appeared in July 4, 1054.

Interestingly, there are concurrent pictographs that appear in China and Japan at the same time as the pictographs in Chaco Canyon, possibly depicting the same supernova. In Japan, the 1054 supernova is described in depth:

> *"According to Japanese texts Mei Getsuki and Ichidai near July 4, 1054 a guest star appeared in the orbit of Orion: It shone like a comet, it was as bright as Jupiter..."*
> (Brandt and Williamson).

The Chinese record is written in *Sung Shih* and it records the supernova was possibly visible for 653 days, as late as the 17th of April, 1056! But it was brightest and located around Taurus on July 4, 1054:

"The star was visible by day like Venus; pointed rays shot out from it on all sides…it was visible for twenty-three days during the day." (Brandt and Williamson).

When comparing the Japanese and Chinese descriptions, the Chinese one of the supernova as having pointed rays shooting from all sides is the most salient piece of evidence tying the supernova pictograph to the supernova of 1054.

An oddity in the world-wide historical record is that although there are extensive descriptions of the supernova of 1054 throughout Asiatic countries, there are no descriptions of this stellar event in European history. Apparently, only a single allusion in Arabic is the only reference to the supernova of 1054 outside of Asian cultures; (Koenig).

Unlike the Chacoans, the Chinese maintained written records:

"We know from Chinese astronomical records that in the year A.D. 1054 there appeared in the sky a bright, but temporary, new 'guest star' that suddenly flared into being and reached a magnitude of about five times brighter than Venus." (Frazier 201).

145

Apparently, the light was so bright that it could be seen during the day for over 23 days. This was the light from what we now call the Crab Nebula.

If the Chacoan supernova pictograph is not a depiction of the supernova, then it is quite a coincidence. There is a hand, a crescent-shaped depiction of the moon, and a star-shaped pictograph.

"From computer studies, astronomers have shown that on the morning of July 4 the Supernova was located only two degrees from the waning crescent moon. The pictograph could be a Chacoan observer's record of those two objects in their temporary proximity." (Frazier 202).

To add to the evidence of the supernova panel, directly below is a faded, but recognizable depiction of a comet blazing across the sky, undoubtedly Halley's Comet.

Furthermore, the supernova pictograph is also in an unusual position, which is on the underside of a cliff overhang. It does not seem accessible from any angle. The artist must have climbed a ladder or otherwise scaled the cliff face to get to this point, or perhaps a long since collapsed perch in the sandstone was available at the time.

Pottery

Nothing is more ubiquitous in the study of Anasazi civilization than the pottery they created, used, and left behind. Chaco Canyon is no exception and evidence of this property is still found in relative abundance. To this day, you can come across pottery sherds in situ around the structures in Chaco. It is hard to comprehend how many millions of pottery bowls, canteens, ollas, ladles, seed jars, mugs, and decorative items must have been created by the Anasazi during the 11 centuries they were the primary occupants of the southwest USA.

With functions for both cooking vessels and water storage, the pottery of Chaco Canyon's most valuable function was likely its ability to store the precious resource of water securely, for long periods. These large pottery vessels for storing water are known as ollas. If the traditional ways extent back to Chacoan times, these ollas would have been carried upon the heads of women as they trekked back and forth from water sources.

While Chaco Canyon is famous for its pottery, scholars estimate most of the pottery in the canyon was actually imported, likely acquired through trade. One possible reason for acquiring these essential pieces of pottery, used for cooking and various types of storage, is that firing clay pottery required the use of large amounts of valuable fuel wood, which was not easy to come by and

Kyle Widner

therefore, it would be considered necessary to use it for the more important tasks of heat and cooking.

There is almost unlimited variety in the shapes and sizes of the bowls, jars, canteens, seed jars, pitchers, etc. Anasazi pottery is documented as being present in the American Southwest from 200 AD on, but pottery at Chaco first appears in 450–500 AD. Settled farmers use ceramics more than nomadic tribes, so it stands to reason as the Chacoans populated the canyon, built permanent structures, and began using agriculture as their primary food source, that the use of pottery would increase, as it is suitable for cooking over a fire and took less time to produce than weaving baskets would require.

While many variations of creating these wares exist, the most common method of making Anasazi pottery was coiling. Unlike most would imagine, a pottery wheel was never used. This is how the process works for this pottery:

Balls of wetted clay are mixed with crushed rock, sand, or crushed pottery (as temper). These are rolled out into long, thin strands. These strands would be added one on top of the other around a base, the sides of the pot getting higher with each strand. The coils were then smoothed by hand or with tools to seal the piece. It should be noted, smoothing tools were not simply utilitarian. It seems the potters took pride not only in their

148

finished wares, but the tools they used as well; smoothing tools inlaid with turquoise and design have been found.

Once the shape of the pot was formed, it was dried then fired. Afterwards, it was decorated.

The Anasazi were masters of firing and decorating pottery. It is amazing that sherds found today, having been exposed to the elements for over a thousand years, yet still retain vibrant colors and patterns. The original colors were likely incredibly bright and well-defined, considering the inevitable dulling that occurs over centuries of sun and blowing sand.

Early pottery was plain and simple, utilitarian in nature, typically called greyware. Simple bowls appeared first, and then larger mouthed vessels used for cooking and food preparation, followed by bigger, narrow-mouthed jars likely used for storing and transporting water. Soon after, other shapes appeared, including animal shapes, gourds, and more elaborate containers with pouring spouts.

Highly artistic, painted pieces came later. At first, the artistic flourishes were combinations of simply painted lines and / or dots, using dark paints that contrasted with the grey body of the pottery. The smooth surface was often covered with a slip—a thin mixture of clay and water—and then painted. Minerals such as iron and plant-based dyes were used for coloration, some applied before firing.

Corrugated pots with banded necks became common, and red on orange and black on red designs began appearing.

When the Anasazi were in full flourish during the Pueblo II / III Periods, regional pottery styles were distinct, seeming competitive in nature as to who could make the brightest, boldest designs. It's also been noted that most of the cooking wares of that time were left corrugated and not smooth, which increased the amount of surface area exposed to the fire when heated. There is no determination as to whether this was intentional or not.

There are 4 common pottery types found in Chaco. These wares are distinguishable from one another in color, texture, type, and patterns.

The first ware is known as "smudged brownware", or simply "brownware". This type of pottery was produced south of Chaco, at the Mogollon Rim area. Although called brownware, the name is misleading, for most of the wares were not actually brown in color. They are highly polished lustrous and shiny bright colors, such as red or orange. This type of ware was constructed out of volcanic clays and it was a reddish color due to the high iron oxide content; (Toll 57). These were considered an exquisite form of pottery and the abundance of smudged brownware sherds found in the refuse mound of pottery sherds in front of Pueblo Alto suggests they were valued in ritual and ceremony.

Redwares are also found, but it is difficult to pinpoint their origin, as they arrived from all over the San Juan Basin, including southeast Utah and northeast Arizona. Although redware was produced over a large geographical area, there was a remarkable consistency to the colors and patterns. Redwares were usually found in open bowl forms, not as closed vessels; (Toll 57). The usual color pattern for redware was a pattern of red and orange, with black lines.

Whitewares are a common, older form of pottery, primarily functional in purpose: bowls and ladles, ollas and canteens, seed jars and jar pitchers; (Toll 57).

Finally, the most abundant pottery found in Chaco is greyware, featuring corrugated sides. Greyware served a purely utilitarian role.

Out of all artifacts found in Chaco, pottery bowls are the fourth most prevalent, just after metates and manos combinations, worked bone, and projectile points. It appears that the remaining bowls were stored for future use, as they are not scattered about, but concentrated in five rooms:

> *"Approximately half of all the whole bowls were excavated from five rooms. Two of these rooms, including the one with the greatest number of specimens, Room 326, had 61 bowls..."* (Neitzel, Artifact Distribution...119).

A less common design was the cylinder vase; it is found only in small numbers, and predominantly is associated with burials. While not known for certain, cylindrical vases were likely high valued for ceremonial use, including rituals that may have involved the chocolate drink imported from Mesoamerica. Out of all the 192 vases excavated from Pueblo Bonito, only 12 of the cylindrical vases were not found in caches or burial rooms; (Crown and Wills 513).

The largest discovery of cylindrical pottery was found in the complex, small burial room known as Room 33. Despite its small size, it seems to be one of the most ornate burial chambers in the southwest. In the chamber with The Turquoise Priest, referred to by Lekson as "The Major Dude", there are about 200 odd cylinder jars. "With a few red-slipped exceptions, all are black-on-white or plain white. Most are Gallup, or Chaco black on white. But painted decoration includes a range of styles..." (Lekson, *The Chaco Meridian*, 87).

As previously mentioned, it is believed the purpose of these cylindrical jars was to hold chocolate drink, an elixir likely limited to use as a ritualistic or ceremonial drink for the upper class. The fact that special vessels were apparently created solely for this purpose lends weight to this theory.

"Among the many unusual objects from Pueblo Bonito are ceramic cylinder jars,

152

vessels typically 2.4 times as tall as they are wide…Fewer than 200 jars are known from the American Southwest, and 166 of these come from Pueblo Bonito. Excavations revealed 111 of these cylindrical jars in a single large cache in one room at the site." (Crown and Hurst 2110).

The cache that is referred is Room 33 of Pueblo Bonito, thus showing that The Turquoise Priest, or The Major Dude, partook in this ceremony. Considering that the dates for the burials in Room 33 are concurrent with the first building phase of Pueblo Bonito, it is reasonable to assume that The Turquoise Priest participated in ceremonies that involved the use of cacao. Lekson comments on the massive amount of cylinder jars and cacao:

"They have a literature all their own…with Mesoamerican implications and refutations…in Mesoamerica, cylinder jars and cacao were high-value items, things nobles would have, but never commoners. The boys at Bonito had both the jars and the cacao." (Lekson 87).

It is possible that The Turquoise Priest traveled from far south, bringing with him Mesoamerican cultural practices? Or he was the son or grandson of a traveler that arrived in Chaco?

***

Kyle Widner

One of the most intriguing ceremonies, at least as far as providing insight into the culture of Ancient Chacoans, is the ritual breakage of pottery. Modern Puebloan oral tradition suggests this is done in order to make it unusable in this world, and send the pot for use in the afterworld. It is apparent, by the ubiquity of pottery sherds, that pottery served a major function in both the spiritual and physical realms.

We know that in many descendant tribes the act of *breaking* pottery is a spiritual rite. As Philip Tuwaletstiwa of the Hopi Tribe says in the Chaco Mystery documentary:

> *"The act of breaking pottery is a way of rendering the pot unusable for the living and sending it to the other worlds."*

The Anasazi elevated pottery to a fine art, perhaps the first fine art of North America. Besides functional use and aesthetic beauty, it has helped serve as a reliable historical record for modern archaeologists. Before tree-ring data was a reliable indicator of construction and occupation dates, Tom Windes used pottery sherds as a reliable predictor of timelines.

> *"Since then, numerous tree-ring dated samples in the 1100-1130 period from Kin Kletso, Pueblo Del Arroyo, and Pueblo Bonito have affirmed this stance. Additionally, supporting evidence comes*

from Pueblo Alto and Bissa'ani. (Windes 19).

There is a large "trash" mound near the Pueblo Alto ruin, high on the cliff above Pueblo Bonito. It is estimated this mound many contain tens of thousands of intentionally broken pots. Was breaking a pot on the pile part of an ancient feasting ceremony? Despite a longing to understand, we simply do not know.

Pottery is the single most in situ distinguishing artifact of the Anasazi culture that is readily available to the modern layman. It is not difficult to find sherds scattered around the ground near ruins, even at tourist friendly parks like Homolovi, just off I-40 near Winslow, Arizona. I found the highest concentrations in Chaco at the Peñasco Blanco and Una Vida ruins.

Wood

"Thousands of timber elements were used in Great House Construction, and it is widely believed that much of this wood was imported from sources far outside the canyon, perhaps 50+ miles away, because there were not enough local trees suitable for building." (Willis et al).

How did these Chacoans transport nearly 240,000 wooden beams from distant mountains? Remember, there were no draft animals, and they did not use the wheel. The roads were constructed later, so we're left to realize this herculean effort was 100% human powered, across irregular, uneven, and unforgiving terrain.

There is evidence that some ponderosa pines existed *in* Chaco Canyon, but it is highly unlikely that they were found in the quantities required for the construction of the Great Houses. The best-known large ponderosa in Chaco was discovered by Neil Judd in the west plaza of Pueblo Bonito, during his excavation in 1924.

"At the south end of the West Court we unexpectedly discovered the remains of a large pine that had stood there, alive and green, when Pueblo Bonito was inhabited. Its decayed trunk lay on the last utilized pavement, and its great, snag-like roots preclude any possibility of its ever having

been removed." (Judd, The Material Culture 3).

Perhaps this tree was an anomaly to the landscape, or was a sacred tree. Judd speculates that it would not be possible for the tree to have been implanted or moved; the root system was far too mature and entwined to have had any disruption.

There would have been a constant need for new beams of consistent size for the construction of the Great Houses and Great Kivas. The planning and logistics of sourcing, selecting, felling, trimming, drying, and hauling, 100% by hand with stone tools, these massive timbers across an unyielding landscape are daunting. No established routes have been found from forest to canyon, and studying the terrain, no obvious paths present themselves.

> *"Cutting and transporting timber may have been the most labor-intensive part of building the great Houses, requiring careful organization to endure a constant supply of new beams."* (Fagan 154).

Neil Judd witnessed a group of 8 Zuni workers carrying a log as their ancestors may have done:

> *"They carried it lengthwise, not cross-wise, supporting it on cross-timbers."* (Fagan 175).

157

We know that the Chacoans stockpiled logs during construction preparation because there are a variety of wood sources that are found within the same building phase, but at different Great Houses. It is likely they gathered many logs, and then selected ones of similar length or girth for uniformity.

> *"Both the Chuskas and San Mateo mountains were being logged simultaneously as early as A.D. 974 and as late as A.D. 1100. There were specific years (cutting dates) when beams from one source area (Chuska Mountains) were incorporated into two great houses (e.g., A.D. 1037: Pueblo Bonito and Pueblo del Arroyo)."* (English et al).

Further:

> *"Likewise, there were specific years when beams from the two sources (Chuska and San Mateo mountains) were incorporated into one great house (e.g., A.D. 1049: Pueblo Bonito). At Pueblo Bonito, one room (room 86) incorporates wood from both the San Mateo and Chuska Mountains cut in A.D. 974."* (English et al).

The wood procurement effort is so intensive that we are forced to think of it as a small army when considering the supply lines involved. These "tree-runners" would have required shoes, food, water, first aid, and shelter during the arduous journey. The woven yucca sandals would have provided only limited protection for the long distance trek over and through the difficult, inhospitable terrain to Chaco.

Up until this point, we have assumed that the "tree-runners" were sent from Chaco to collect the logs and return with them. Perhaps the reverse was true, and the Chacoans simply traded for them, as they were required.

> *"Tree harvesters may have been residents of the Chuska Mountains, rather than Chaco Canyon, which would have eliminated many of the scheduling problems associated with long-distance procurement of timbers."* (Cameron and Toll 12).

Possibly, their distant logging camps were Chacoan inspired communities, or perhaps clans, who lived within these distant forests. These mountain acclimated specialists could have logged the trees, dried them out, and transported the massive beams from the mountains to Chaco and returned with trade goods.

The logistics involved boggle the imagination. Anyone who has hiked this section of New Mexico knows the terrain is less than ideal, to put it mildly. When the phrase "from 50+ miles away" is mentioned, that is a straight line. And there are precious few areas in the Chaco part of the world where you can walk in a straight line for very long. Our imagination can supply endless possibilities, but we will likely never know the reality.

Construction and Labor

If Chaco were simply a collection of small pueblo stone houses, scattered through the canyon, it would be unremarkable—and common. Pueblo villages from the Anasazi period are strewn across the Colorado Plateau.

In Chaco Canyon, multiple projects of mammoth scope and size took place, their ghostly, hulking shells remain today for us to walk in and around.

How were these massive projects conceived and their resources organized? Who were the architects, engineers, and workers? Did the knowledge and technology come from outside the canyon or was there an "Anasazi Einstein" who was born and drove the boom?

Managing everything required for projects of this scope requires engineered plans, sourcing of resources, skills, delegation, duties, tools, and training of workers. Additional considerations include accommodations, supplies, food, compensation, and water for the workers. These laborers either wanted to perform the labor because it achieved a desired end, or they were coerced by some other powerful means to partake in such an intensive process.

Studying the complexity of Chacoan construction, it is hard to arrive at any conclusion that does not involve strong leadership. These leaders would have known what the project entailed in its full scope, and then organized the labor efforts. This would have required a thorough

Kyle Widner

understanding of the plans created by the previous generation, possibly generations prior. And all with no written language?

First, let's take a practical look at how knowledge was accumulated and passed in this era. Knowing that there was no written language means there were no written records, plans or blueprints to refer to. Thus, the knowledge had to be passed by examples and / or oral tradition, which is notoriously unreliable. Remember the childhood game "Telephone"?

"Telephone" is a game played around the world, in which one person whispers a message to another, which is passed through a group of people until the last player announces the message back to the first player. Errors accumulate in the retellings, so the statement announced by the last player almost always differs significantly, and often amusingly, from the first.

How do these messages get "lost in translation"? There are many reasons, including anxiousness or impatience, erroneous corrections, the difficult-to-master art of listening correctly, and that some players may deliberately alter what is being said to influence decision making, or inject a personal bias. While all of these reasons can lend to amusement in a game among friends, when it comes to constructing 4 story buildings that consist of hundreds of rooms, we can see how the oral relaying of messages could lead to problems.

Kyle Widner

One possible reason for the huge numbers of kivas in Chaco is that they were instruction rooms, for the passing on of accumulated knowledge. The apprentices would sit, taking instruction from the experienced masons, hunters, builders, etc., who would teach them as they had been taught. They likely understood how this hands-on approach to transferring knowledge resulted in a better outcome than teaching via the "Telephone" method. In addition to the classroom setting, the apprentices would have practiced and applied the teachings repeatedly, ensuring they understood them thoroughly, until such time when they became the master and were preparing to train their own apprentice.

The knowledge and skills lead to something big, for someone or a group of skilled leaders, in which they saw the potential that made the Great Houses possible. The individual or group that conceived this plan would have had an ability to organize on the highest of levels, relaying the plans effectively to those that would be relied on to carry them out.

At the dawn of the Chaco Phenomenon, the stunning speed of technological change is dazzling. What change in societal structure suddenly inspired an ancient desert-dwelling society to evolve from communities of pit-houses into a sophisticated building boom of 4story buildings consisting of 700 rooms each? To answer these questions, we can look to four possible models that would support organizing this gigantic effort.

1. **A purely communal model or organization**
This would have been based on the societal structure of modern Puebloan descendants of the Anasazi, which do not adhere to a hierarchal societal structure. The modern day Pueblo is peaceful, egalitarian society. There is no evidence that this societal structure has ever been invoked with projects of a scope comparable to the Chacoan buildings. Stephen Lekson speaks of how the modern Puebloan descendants are indeed a peaceful egalitarian society, and that this modern model evolved from the Puebloan rejection of the Chaco model. Unsurprisingly, there are other opinions:

> "The Chaco Canyon ceremonials and related work projects may have been hyper-potluck affairs, in which a central authority probably coordinated contributions from different locales based on available opportunities and institutional requirements." (Earle 33).

Dr. R. Gwinn Vivian does not believe there was any sort of hierarchy that subordinated the small house communities to the Great Houses. He asserts that there were two separate cultures co-existing in Chaco Canyon:

> "I argue that the observed settlement and architectural variability in the

Kyle Widner

Chaco Core is organizationally meaningful but does not reflect the structure of a single hierarchically organized society. There are other theories about the management of labor at Chaco. Some assert that hierarchies may have existed, but that they were not well-defined: 'We agreed that there must have been leaders in Chaco Canyon to organize the construction of great houses and roads, but their status was not highly marked. In fact, their power may have been situational, emerging only in the context of communal activities.'" (Cameron and Toll 11).

Therefore, although there was organization, it may have been less defined than that of modern management. What this means is that the Chacoans could have had *linear* management, where all people had a role, but no role was necessarily subjugated to another. Or, Brian Fagan theorizes that there may have been a division of labor based on clans and kin groups with obligations placed on extended families and households; (Fagan 147). Fagan continues to describe how all of the family's talents would have assisted both the building of Chaco and the trade with other far off clans. Women would have been primary contributors to

Kyle Widner

the construction effort, a point that is often overlooked.

However, in this model, someone or some persons, needed to hold the master plan, and be a final decision making authority. Could this have been a committee, a collaborative effort that made decisions by consensus?

2. The volunteer boss and voluntary worker

Let us explore the possibility of those who were happy to work participating in these big projects. As an example, consider the construction of the Hoover Dam on the Colorado River in the 1930s.

The option to be able to work on the Great Houses could have been exchanged for security, food, water, and the ability to live in a good community, similarly to the construction of my adopted hometown of Boulder City, Nevada, which was originally a government camp to house the builders of Hoover Dam. In other words, the construction of the Great Houses could have provided the equivalent of good paying jobs. It may have been a coveted position during Anasazi times, to be a Chacoan builder, log-runner, or mason.

Chacoan feats of architecture took the cooperative interaction of many people, over many years, with resources required from far-flung regions. Logically, a structure had to be in place for planning, managing, and funding these efforts. Possibly, like the building of Hoover Dam, these jobs were highly anticipated, highly coveted, and attracted plentiful labor and expertise to Chaco.

3. Power bosses and voluntary, but coerced workers

Think of American "company towns" in the 1800s. Occasionally, company towns emerged from a paternalistic effort to create a utopian workers community. Town halls, schools, libraries, and other central services were provided by the company in order to build strong communities and help make workers more productive. Bars or places of ill repute were banned.

In others manifestations, large companies had less idealistic goals. At many factories or other industrial sites with large concentrations of workers, the remoteness and lack of public transportation prevented workers from leaving for other jobs. A "company store" with exploitive prices and limited selection would be the only source of goods. In some cases, workers earned only "script", which could be spent only at the company store. Workers could take credit at the company store, and often ended up indebted to the companies they worked for. Could a similar model of exploiting workers have been employed in Chaco? Perhaps the Great Houses were the company towns of this time.

Kyle Widner

4. Owners and slaves

This is the darkest of our four options for organizational structure at Chaco. As a template, lets equate to the Egyptian pyramids, the builders of which employed armies of slaves to construct the great pyramids. Could bands of slave traders have captured workers from small, local Anasazi communities, and enslaved them to work on the Great Houses, feeding them starvation rations, and disposing of them when they were no longer able to work? While there is no evidence to support this theory, it has been postulated by some who have studied other Native American tribes who did practice enslavement of competing tribes.

Whatever the division of labor was, it still required massive organizational efforts for both labor and material, and this effort was eventually successful. Consider Mary Metcalf's calculation of labor hours involved in the construction of Pueblo Bonito:

> *" 'My calculations indicate that approximately 805,000 person hours were required to build Pueblo Bonito…' and at Chetro Ketl, an estimated 500,000 person hours. Both Pueblo Bonito and Chetro Ketl took the longest to construct, are the largest and have the most man hours. The lowest investment of hours that a Great House took to construct is Kin Kletso, with just 130,000 estimated man hours."* (Metcalf 77).

To add complexity, multiple Great Houses were worked on simultaneously, multiplying the resources and labor required.

The Abandonment of Chaco

With the stunning amount of labor and resources that went into building Chaco, one can only beg the question: why abandon it?

When one hears about the Anasazi who "vanished", it means the general abandonment of the Colorado Plateau around the year 1300 AD. The abandonment of Chaco was different; it was an orderly migration back to the Mesa Verde area, and occurred in approximately 1150 AD.

Migration was not a new concept to southwestern peoples; it was a way of life for their Anasazi brethren before, during, and after the Chaco period. The entire Colorado Plateau is littered with the final resting places of pit-houses, pueblos, caves, and cliff dwellings that were only occupied for a generation or two. Chaco had a stunning run of over 12 generations, very long by Anasazi standards. They survived droughts and environmental challenges, periods of scarce resources, and seemingly lived without violence for those 2+ centuries. And then, for reasons that can only be speculated upon, they slowly and deliberately sealed the Great Houses, ceremonially dismantled and burned the kivas and Great Kivas, and left.

It is true a great drought descended on the San Juan River Basin in 1130-1180, and that could have been a factor in the decision to migrate away. But these people had survived multiple severe droughts through the centuries; why would this one be the sole reason for leaving? Perhaps other factors were at play, and the drought served as the "final straw".

Most civilizations end by either eroding from the inside out, or conquest by a stronger enemy. There is no evidence of warfare at Chaco, although the sealed doors, and reduced entry points to the Great Houses were once thought to be evidence of defensive measures against external enemies. Today it is generally accepted the doors were filled with masonry, and the kivas burned over a generation as a ceremonial cleansing, signifying the closing or sealing of whatever occurred at Chaco.

Without conquest by an outside enemy, that leaves an internal rotting of society as a leading suspect. Was there an increasing disparity between the rich and poor that reached a tipping point? Did trade with the south dry up and leave Chaco with reduced prestige? Did the outlying communities that supplied food to Chaco suffer agricultural calamity or did they collectively revolt against the leadership?

Genetically, the current Pueblo tribes of the Rio Grande, Hopi, and Zuni, show ties to the Chacoan-era Anasazi. The descendant Pueblo tribes today are all located within 100 miles of Chaco, mostly to the southeast, the Zuni about 85 miles to the south / southwest, and the Hopi 142 miles to the west. The Chacoans migrated back to the Mesa Verde area about 1150, and in 1300 the general abandonment by the Anasazi across the Colorado Plateau occurred, the descendant tribes eventually establishing themselves permanently in their current locations.

Whatever occurred in Chaco, the Anasazi nor their descendants, ever returned. Modern oral tradition suggests a mixed relationship with the memory of Chaco. Some view it with reverence and an important place and time in their history. Some view it as a place where unnatural things happened, and it was sealed, rejected, and abandoned intentionally.

Water, Dams, and Irrigation

Visitors to Chaco are immediately entranced by the ruins of the Great Houses, and with good reason. They are stately, regal, and mysterious. But perhaps the most important, life-sustaining feat of engineering and construction is not easily visible to the modern tourist.

A sophisticated system of check dams, ditches, irrigation canals, and gridded fields existed to capture and exploit the runoff of the rainfall from the high cliff walls and smaller side canyons. These smaller side canyons would funnel large volumes of rainwater from thunderstorms, turning them into violent, short-lived torrents of water crashing down into the canyon.

A check dam is a small dam constructed across a waterway to collect, store, or re-direct water. In terrains such as Chaco, violent summer rainstorms strike suddenly, and everything changes just as suddenly. For the Anasazi, water would have come roaring down the side of the canyon, flooding agricultural fields and destroying crops. However, with a check dam, this could be avoided, and the water, while detrimental in flood, could be collected and used wisely.

When the rains exploded from the skies, the women leapt into action. They would take empty ollas to the pools of collected rainwater, fill their jars, store them safely, and repeat until the water supply had been replenished.

After the rains passed, and fields began to dry, they would open the check dam temporarily, to allow water to flow into the fields and serve the thirsty crops.

> *"Formal rectangular plots for planting maize and other food crops in flood irrigated farms existed especially on the north side of the Chaco Canyon...the best known example of this type of farming is the Chetro Ketl fields...approximately twenty acres of land were leveled and then divided by low soil ridges into individual plots measuring roughly seventy-five by forty-five feet."* (Vivian and Hilpert 138).

There were also canals, which ran between the set rectangular plots, allowing for a controlled amount of water to enter into each plot.

> *"Water control in Chaco core involved a specialized irrigation...the canyon has no flowing water, therefore, runoff from thunderstorms were collected and diverted to the fields from side canyons..."* (Vivian and Hilpert 288-89).

The summer monsoons would have been critical for agricultural success. As the crops grew, a steady supply of water would have been very important. The Chacoan system of check dams, irrigation ditches, and gridded fields was effective in allocating water for agriculture.

"This type of water control occurs consistently on the north side of the canyon from Mockingbird Canyon on the east of Escavada Wash...on the south side of the canyon only two water control systems have been found: one near Casa Rinconada, and one near Peñasco Blanco." (Vivian and Hilpert 289).

There have been many dams found across the canyon, and likely many more that have been washed out or eroded away by time and flooding. Some of these structures were not trivial in size. The largest dam excavated was located at the bottom of Cly Canyon, a tributary canyon of Chaco Canyon:

"It dammed the runoff from Cly Canyon...and directed the water through a 3 ½ -foot wide gate near the center of the dam into a canal. The dam was more than 120 feet long, 20 feet thick, and stood at least seven feet high." (Frazier 101).

"The Chaco irrigation system incorporates developed seeps and springs, small stone check dams across minor drainages, large earthen dams, water diversion devices, storage tanks, agricultural terraces and garden plots..." (Lister and Lister 140).

While we are justifiably impressed by the "greatness" of the architecture, Great Houses, and kivas in Chaco, their advanced system of collecting and allocating the single most precious resource in Chaco was a critical component of their success.

Mysteries

Almost every question about Chaco answered generates more questions. This section contains some of the key questions that have gone unsolved.

Why choose Chaco Canyon to settle?
Inhospitable terrain, not near any resources, little water, difficult soil for agriculture, brutal climate, little rainfall. This is the most common, unanswerable question. It promotes speculation of a spiritual or ritualistic connection to the area, first and foremost.

What was the purpose of the Great Houses?
Chacoans built very large, multi-story buildings, with very little evidence of habitation, and very few hearths for heating or cooking. Were they designed to impress or intimidate, and house only a few elites, similar to the Vatican? Were they trade facilities, used for storage? Whatever their purpose, they were a focal point of Chaco and a draw to the residents of surrounding communities.

Why so many kivas?
Did each clan or influential family have their own kiva? Were they learning centers, work rooms, storage facilities, and ceremonial centers? Great Kivas could hold up to 400 people at one time. Were these arenas, community centers, feasting or ceremonial structures with elaborate rituals?

Who was buried in Room 33 of Pueblo Bonito? What was their status?

These skeletons are obviously of a different stature or class. Specifically, the one I refer to as The Turquoise King is unusual in many ways; taller, older, with better nutrition and buried with a fortune in goods. Was he Anasazi, or did he come from another culture?

Why did the Anasazi seal the doors and windows of the Great Houses, then burn the kivas, and then leave Chaco Canyon?

A slow sealing up of Chaco occurred over more than a generation. They took great care to seal doors and windows, disassemble and burn the kivas. Was this a ritual designed to capture and seal an evil presence, or did environmental factors like drought or agricultural failure cause them to move on, and if so, why hang around and spend the time and resources to seal everything? We do know a massive, crippling drought occurred in 1130-1180, which probably hastened any decision.

How did trade with Mesoamerica work?

The Chacoans had scarlet macaws from Central America, chocolate (nearest cocoa tree is 1200 miles away), copper bells, and seashells from the coast of Mexico. Goods obviously flowed into Chaco, leading us to wonder if there were regular trading caravans and outposts. What goods went back to Mesoamerica in these trades?

What was the organizational structure of Chacoan society?

Was it peaceful and egalitarian, like the modern Puebloans? Or were the Anasazi living there enslaved and forced to build the massive structures? Possibly, the Great

Houses and Great Kivas were public works projects such as the Hoover Dam.

Was there outside influence that led to the fluorescence?

How did the Chacoans go from pit-house and small pueblo living to building the biggest structures in North America until the invention of steel? A major influx of technology and engineering talent was either imported or there was a massive, rapid, and organic development of skills.

Why was the east side of Pueblo Bonito built ever closer to Threatening Rock?

They built Pueblo Bonito under a massive, dangerous slab of sandstone they knew was going to fall. We know this because they tried propping it up and reinforcing it. It eventually fell in 1941, destroying the northeast quadrant of Pueblo Bonito. Was it an act of faith to live under the threat?

Why track the 18.6 year cycle of the moon?

The Sun Dagger on Fajada Butte was capable of tracking the solstices and equinoxes, key to timing agriculture planting and harvesting. But why did it also track the 18.6year cycle of lunar standstills? Were they searching for some key to predicting climate or weather cycles?

All Roads lead to Chaco? 30' wide, hundreds of miles, connecting?

The roads required massive effort to build, and were over-engineered and underused. Did they serve a ritual or ceremonial function? Were they trying to communicate with gods?

Why so few burials present?

Just over 300 burials have been found in the canyon that was occupied by Chacoans for over 200 years. Where are the dead? Advanced ground penetrating radar reveals no clues to any undiscovered graveyard. No funeral pyres or cremation sites have been discovered.

How did they cut down, trim, and transfer 240,000 logs by hand?

The nearest forest of ponderosa pine trees is over 50 miles from Chaco. The building of the Great Houses and Great Kivas demanded logs of uniform size. Without draft animals or the wheel, these logs were felled, trimmed, dried, and carried by hand across very unforgiving, difficult terrain. They did not have metal tools; everything was accomplished with stone tools.

Why are buildings perfectly aligned with the sun and / or moon?

Many buildings in Chaco Canyon have obvious solar and lunar alignments, and some buildings have alignments with each other. There are likely many alignments yet to be discovered or understood. Most famous of the alignments is the north / south wall in Chaco, whose shadow disappears uniformly at high noon each day. Why such strict adherence to these alignments?

Why did they not learn, or choose *not* to use the wheel?

The Anasazi of Chaco Canyon were obviously incredibly talented and brilliant engineers. Why did they never discover or use the wheel? Or did they, and view it as not very useful in the terrain in which they lived?

Why did they not develop a written language, despite the use of petroglyphs?

They obviously used symbols, pecked into the rocks or painted onto the sandstone cliffs. Why did they never apply this to moveable stones, plates, or write on plant leaves, cloth, etc?

Petroglyphs: by pecking away at the "desert varnish" that accumulates on sandstone surfaces, the Anasazi created petroglyphs on many rocks and cliff faces throughout the southwest. Many have been damaged or "added to" via vandalism.

What was the role of cacao / chocolate?

The nearest cocoa tree is 1200 miles from Chaco. But chocolate residue has been found in cylinder mugs in

180

Pueblo Bonito. Was chocolate a ceremonial drink, with a caffeine buzz? Or for the elite class only?

Were the sun dagger slabs already in place, or did the Chacoans arrange them?

Three massive sandstone slabs on Fajada Butte create slivers of light that penetrate and mark the seasons on petroglyphs pecked into the cliff wall. Were these three stones shaped and placed to create the sun dagger effect, or did they already exist, and did generations of Sun Priests watch closely, and peck the petroglyph to match?

What was function of the stone circles on North Canyon rim?

Mysterious man made circles, without a known purpose.

Does the supernova panel represent the Crab Nebula supernova of July 4, 1054?

Near Peñasco Blanco, a pictograph suggests a bright light in the sky, near a moon in correct phase for the date. Is this a recording of that supernova, and if it is, what was the significance of it to them, was it simply recoding history, a warning, or an omen?

Does the pictograph on the supernova panel represent Halley's Comet?

Just below the supernova pictograph, the faint remains of what looks like a comet exist. Halley's Comet appeared just a few years after the 1054 supernova. Did they record this, as well, in the same spot?

What was the purpose of the Pueblo Alto "mound of pottery"?

Near Pueblo Alto, there is a huge refuse mound that contains massive amounts of broken pottery, most of which appears to have been intentionally broken. Was this part of a ritual, for example at the conclusion of a feast, where intentionally broken pots were given to relatives already in the afterworld?

Kyle Widner

Part Three: What Happened in Chaco Canyon?

A Personal Interpretation

While based on historical fact, this third and final part of the book is a work of fiction. It incorporates my own interpretation of the available research, a reading between the lines of contemporary Puebloan oral tradition, and what I can best describe as my intuition about what occurred over 1,000 years ago. Responsibility for any and all instances of error, omission, conflicts with reality, or generalized ignorance is borne solely by the author.

Was it the Rise and Fall of Chaco, or Fall and Rise?

The Anasazi were loose bands of hunter-gatherers, agriculturalists, and hardy survivors in the difficult landscape of the modern four corners area of Utah, Colorado, Arizona, and New Mexico. They took advantage of the meager subsistence the Colorado Plateau offered, living in caves, pit-houses, and simple stone structures created from the earth around them. Over thousands of years, they migrated as weather patterns and resources ebbed and flowed, favoring one area for a time, and then another.

They had no known human enemies, living mostly in peace without the need for offensive or defensive warfare. Population densities were small enough that conflict over terrain seldom arose. Without the need for centralized leadership to coordinate war or defend resources from enemies, an egalitarian society naturally formed, without strong leaders or heavy-handed authority.

Despite the lack of enemies, they faced one constant foe, one persistent life and death struggle: water. Much of the Colorado Plateau is arid, with frustratingly little predictability. Rain is never consistent, either in quantity or location. Years of dry weather can be washed away in the violent torrent of a single summer thunderstorm.

During this long period of existence, the Anasazi lived simply, unremarkably, with major changes coming slowly. Key advancements came in the form of the introduction of willow baskets, which were lined with

Kyle Widner

pinyon sap to form a waterproof seal, a few new agricultural crops, adoption of the bow and arrow, and learning to fire pottery. Life expectancy was short; drought and hunger threatened more years than not. It was not unlike Stone Age existence in other parts of the planet.

And then suddenly, in one non-descript, barren corner of the Anasazi world now called Chaco Canyon, their world changed forever, changes that reverberate to this day.

In the 9th century, a strange wind foreshadowed an even stranger turn of events. Children were running around and chasing the dogs and turkeys playfully, laughing and having fun; occasionally gently scolded by a mother cooking or a father skinning hides in preparation for the coming cold winter.

On the tails of that mysterious wind came a group of strange people, making their way north from the far, far south—an area known as Mesoamerica. The children stopped and watched, the older ones brave and curious, standing tall to watch these men draped in bright colors approach from the distance. The smaller children, not understanding, ran to their mothers and fathers and stood behind them, poking their small heads out from around from their protective shelter to take a look. Their eyes wide and their mouths slightly open, for they had never seen anything like this before.

These people were tall, almost 6'0", while most of the local men were about 5'4" and the women about 5'0".

These strangers were dressed in unique robes made of colorful feathers, and carried themselves upright and dignified, like royalty. They carried nothing, but had several servants behind them, each carrying large bundles. Attempts at introductions in unfamiliar languages, followed by various common hand gestures, formed the basis for communication, and led to an offer to stay and rest.

This group brought unique items with them, treasures unlike anything the occupants of Chaco had ever seen before: brightly colored macaw feathers, seashells, copper bells, and chocolate drink made from cocoa. The local Chacoans were awed and impressed. But even more impressive were the skills the strangers brought from their kingdom to the south; engineering, logistics, astronomy, architecture, building, and jewelry making. Also, the strangers carried a dark secret: knowledge of a class system in which the few ruled the many. Being egalitarian in nature, the Anasazi were completely unaware of this concept.

Seeking a kingdom of their own and rule, the strangers had fled from their fiefdom in Mesoamerica, and the corrupt nepotistic leaders that held them back from their ambitions. They could not return, for they would surely be put to death for treason. They were masters at their crafts and skills, and would be sorely missed, but leaving was a one-way ticket. They had to succeed here or perish.

By using manipulative tactics that would make Machiavelli proud, the strangers quickly began using their advanced knowledge and exotic goods to create a control structure and position themselves as the leaders of the Chacoans. As these Anasazi did not seem to aspire to any goals other than a simple life, the strangers sought out a common enemy to advance their cause, but these people did not seem to have enemies.

However, they changed tact, and quickly hit upon the one thing the Anasazi wanted more than anything else: consistent rains. The strangers saw how the locals watched the sun and moon, referring to "Father Sky" and marveling at how predictable everything was in the heavens. But the locals also looked as the environment on earth around them, "Mother Earth", and lamented at how unpredictable she was, especially with the life-giving rains.

Serving their own purposes with surreptitious intent, they convinced the Chacoans that if they built massive Great Houses with many rooms, and aligned them perfectly with the sun and moon, it would be an invitation for Father Sky to come and live in harmony with Mother Earth. To help, the strangers would live in these Great Houses and communicate directly with Father Sky on behalf of the Chacoans.

After overcoming the language barrier and learning the local tongue quickly, the builders began to teach advanced building skills to the local workforce. At the same time, engineers evaluated the materials available for construction and made plans for the collection of necessary materials. To placate the people being taken away from their normal work, seashell jewelry and macaw feathers were used as payment and rewards. They were highly valued by the Chacoans, who had never seen such exotic goods.

Thus the deliberate process of subjugation began. The new leaders selected the most beautiful of the local girls as wives, plied their fathers and mothers with exotic gifts, sips of chocolate elixir, and the promise of a better life for them and their daughter. This began a ruling class by matriarchal lineage, with the lucky blood relatives of those married into the system showered with favors. For generations, they built and bred mostly within their own class, contrary to centuries of Anasazi tradition.

They set up a system of apprenticeship, selecting the most promising of the locals for participation in the building projects. These students were better fed and clothed than the other locals, and added to the power of the new rulers, who now chose winners and losers from the local populace. Families were left to curry favor with the rulers, trying to get their sons and daughters accepted.

The massive building projects got underway. To build the Great Houses, they organized teams that traveled 50-100 miles away on foot to chop down 60' ponderosa pines with stone axes and carry them back to Chaco Canyon by hand, as the Anasazi had no metal tools, did not use the wheel, and had no domesticated draft animals. Eventually, they made deals with the tribes that lived closest to these forests, and taught them to deliver these logs on a regular basis. They were paid in jewelry, exotic gifts, and the privilege of participating in Chacoan rituals. All these forms of payment held great appeal to the curious

Anasazi, who were drawn to the canyon by its growing influence and power.

Specialized teams mined sandstone from the cliff faces and crafted them to fit the walls of the Great Houses. Over the generations, unique patterns were developed. Some of these were functional to help make stronger, more durable walls, but some were purely aesthetic, a statement of style, if you will.

When the rulers became concerned they would run out of seashells and feathers they used as payment and motivation, they devised a two-part plan. First, they had discovered the local source of turquoise, which they quickly learned to shape and polish into beautiful necklaces, bracelets, pendants, earrings, and beads. Anyone caught with turquoise not finished by the Chacoan jewelers was banished from Chaco, allowing them to control the supply with an iron grip. These finished turquoise pieces were highly valued by the locals, and served as the most valuable of currency items. Secondly, they loaded up some of the servants with this turquoise jewelry and sent them back to the south to trade for scarlet macaw feathers, copper bells, more seashells, and cocoa. The servants returned with a surprise; they brought back several mating pairs of macaws, alive in cages. This spectacle further served their needs, with a ready supply of the valuable feathers to craft goods and to exchange. Groups of traders arriving and leaving became a regular sight in Chaco.

Over the subsequent generations, their Chaco kingdom became well established. The Anasazi had been subjugated, the Great Houses were massive, monumental temples that the rulers lived in, and provided storage for the massive wealth they had accumulated. Traders came and went, and they beheld the Great Houses in awe. With no enemies, no standing army was required, freeing more resources for building the opulent temples to the ruling class.

And the promised, consistent rains the new rulers had promised when Father Sky was invited to live with Mother Earth? They had gotten amazingly lucky early on in the process, after the first major portion of Pueblo Bonito was completed, and many years of good rains followed. When bad years inevitably returned, the rulers convinced them it was the lack of effort and faith that caused the drought. More great buildings were needed for Father Sky, if he was going to return and help Mother Earth.

As generations passed, the power of the ruling class grew and rituals and ceremonies were devised to accent the power of the rulers. Chocolate drink in special, ceremonial cylinders was said to offer the power of the spirits. These locals had never experienced caffeine before, and the drink did indeed seem to bring special powers. By sharing the drink only with compliant locals, divisions in class and favor grew within the ranks. Jealousy, an emotion once unfamiliar to the locals, created friction and conflict, as the Anasazi fell further and further away from their traditional egalitarian system.

Building multi-story structures had never been done before, and it awed the locals. The further up they built, the closer they were to the heavens and Father Sky. One clan of the ruling class was the Sky Priests. One particular Sky Priest had a pet project. High on a nearby butte, he noticed the play of sunlight and moonlight on the sandstone wall behind three huge fallen slabs of rock. A sharp dagger of light would appear near the middle of the day and dance away as the sun moved across the sky. The Sky Priest began marking the play of light at various points every day, an incredibly monotonous and persistent task that he passed on to his sons, until one day, a grandson took note of the patterns of Father Sky.

Now, they knew the moment when the days would be getting longer, when they would get shorter, and the exact halfway points in between. This information became extremely valuable in deciding when to plant and harvest crops and tracking the seasonal migrations of wild game. The special rituals and ceremonies that accompanied these events were designed to honor the ruling class and therefore help them remain in power. (This "Sun Dagger" was discovered by artist Anna Sofaer in 1977.)

Pueblo Bonito, the name of the mightiest Great House, continued to be built, re-built, and remodeled, expanding toward the east where a massive sandstone monolith, already detached from the northern cliff face, loomed ominously above. If it fell, it would easily take out a quarter or more of Pueblo Bonito, and make the balance of the building unstable. The rulers told the locals it was an act of faith, if they were faithful to the rulers and their plans, Mother Earth would keep this "threatening rock" in place. To help, they put up braces and ritualistic offerings. It worked, as it did not fall until 1941.

The influence of Chaco grew and grew, with outlying communities springing up to the north, west, and south. Mostly farmers and traders, these groups wanted the prestige and access to Chaco that living close by would bring. They would deliver food, pottery, and wood; and receive jewelry, exotic goods like macaw feathers, and if especially fortunate, be able to participate in the chocolate drink ritual. When large amounts of labor were required for construction and the other tasks, workers could be drawn from these communities, for they all longed to receive the goods that their rulers could offer.

Grumblings among the Anasazi began to grow, as the promised pacification of Mother Earth never seemed to come to pass. Once again, the rulers got lucky. Their Sky Priest was able to predict when a solar eclipse would occur. Using this knowledge, they explained that Father Sky was angry with them for their lack of effort and progress in building his home on Mother Earth. To show his anger, he was going to darken the daytime sky. With a dramatic and somber ceremony, they gathered the frightened locals together, and as the moon slipped in front of the sun, and the sky darkened, their power was further cemented. This was proof to them that the rulers did indeed communicate with Father Sky.

To further temper the lack of consistent rains, the rulers introduced a new system of collecting water. The rulers had long observed the huge rainfalls that were common in summer, in which huge downpours would be followed by massive runoff from the top of the cliff tops. They watched carefully, and then directed the building of a system of dams and canals to irrigate the corn, beans, and squash, and allow the locals to refill their large pottery jugs, known as ollas, with water. This, they claimed, was Father Sky trying to help as best he could, but the locals were still not doing enough. The Anasazi were growing weary, but had no other choice. They continued on with their lives.

One midsummer day, everyone in the canyon received an unexpected shock. Suddenly, in the sky, a second sun appeared, and remained for 23 days, visible day and night. The Sky Priest stammered and stumbled as he tried to explain this unexpected phenomenon. The people could see that the rulers had no idea what was happening, and it frightened them. It was the beginning of what would become a large break in the faith of the rulers, and the awe in which the locals held them. To warn future generations of the second sun, a painting of it was placed on the rocks near the mouth of the canyon. This artist painted the position and phase of the moon at the time of the second sun. (July 4, 1054, a supernova that became the Crab Nebula was visible on earth. Chinese astronomical records verify it, and the "supernova panel" remains in Chaco today.)

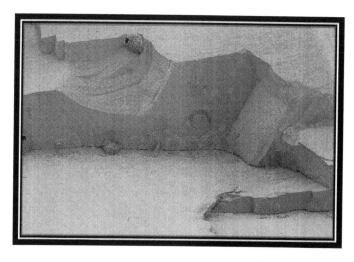

Supernova Panel: the supernova of July 4, 1054, now known as the Crab Nebula, is memorialized in this pictograph painted on the underside of the cliff near Peñasco Blanco, at the west end of Chaco Canyon. The moon phase and position in relation to the supernova has been confirmed to be correct for the date. Barely visible below the star and moon, is a faded yellow representation of what is believed to be Halley's Comet.

The expanding ruling class remained living in the Great Houses surrounded by immense treasures they ruthlessly accumulated for themselves. These were not for use by the regular Anasazi, but for the benefit of only the ruling class, parceled out to receive more corn and luxury goods. Corn was considered the best food available, and the ruling class began to consume more and more of it, excluding other foods like squash, beans, and animal meat, all now considered foods of the lower class.

A diet with too much corn and not enough of the other essential amino acids causes mental disturbance, a condition known as Pellagra. Corn, squash, and beans, combined with wild game, have all the essential amino acids and dietary iron, essentially a balanced diet. This corn-heavy diet, combined with the predictable results of rampant inbreeding among the ruling class, led to instability in decision-making. Acting irrationally and ruling with increasing ruthlessness, the occupants of the Great Houses became paranoid, and began restricting entrance into the Great Houses to one or two points.

The Great House occupants lived in increasingly opulent wealth while the common Anasazi became little more than indentured servants. Even though the rains had not stabilized as the rulers had promised, the caste system was fully in place, and the Chaco Anasazi had not rebelled against it. Yet.

In their circular, underground kivas, oral traditions from centuries ago continued to be passed down, just as the Anasazi had always done, for it was part of their traditions. Many of these stories had carried the messages of the past, of the Anasazi way. So much had been lost in Chaco, they hardly recognized their modern world when compared to what had sustained them before. This realization spread amongst the people, and they felt a strong desire to return to the old ways, but felt hopeless to resist.

Finally, they could take no more. After 11 generations, the rulers had grown fat, lazy, rich, slovenly, cruel, inbred, and racked with effects of Pellagra. A great drought began in 1130, putting a final nail in the dream and fantasy of consistent rains.

The game was up; angry mobs of Anasazi grabbed sticks and began yelling at the rulers, demanding they get out. The rulers were driven out, repudiated and shunned by angry Chacoans. Mother Earth was now dryer than ever and it was the fault of these charlatans, who drove them from their ancient way of life, and now it was time to go back to living in peace with each other, equally. Mother Earth had sustained them before, and she would again.

Descendants of the original strangers were now viewed as a manifestation of a curse, bad medicine, an evil force that had led the Anasazi people away from their core principals, a siren calling them with promises of utopia with regular rains, only to eventually realize they had been lured to crash upon the rocks. The Anasazi now fully rejected this new way, and vowed to return to their ancient path.

Over the course of the next generation, after kicking the rulers out, they used masonry to seal the windows and doors of the Great Houses with great care, disassembled and burnt the kivas, and began a slow migration back to the Mesa Verde area. It was not a rushed abandonment, it occurred slowly and deliberately. This could have taken as much effort as their creation, but the burning was a ceremonial cleansing and a permanent, final closing of this bad chapter.

Returning to Mesa Verde, the migration complete by the mid 1100's, they were greeted with new problems in their old lands. Violent bands of Indian raiders were migrating down from the north and finding the Anasazi easy targets, stealing their food. The Anasazi were forced off the mesa tops and valleys and into defensive structures in the cliff walls. What was left of the Chacoan architectural and building knowledge was used to construct these defensive cliff houses across Mesa Verde and much of the four corners region.

In about 1258, a massive volcanic eruption in Indonesia, eight times bigger than the Krakatoa eruption, altered the climate over much of the planet. This would have discolored the Anasazi sky, shortened the growing season, and created food shortages. As the food supply dwindled, the Anasazi would have been eating further down the food chain, including deer mice, a source of Haute Virus, which is deadly. All this was compounded by another great drought that began in 1276 and lasted until 1299.

It all became too much for the dwindling, weakened, and dispirited population of the Anasazi to take. They were being attacked, and were hungry. Some were dying for unknown reasons. The sky was displaying unusual colors, and bad omens appeared everywhere. When the great drought began to punish the land in 1276, they tried to hold out, but could not any longer. Drought affected not only their drinking and cooking water, but also their ability to grow food, and also drove away the wild game and wilted the wild plant food sources.

About 1300, the remaining Anasazi uniformly abandoned the Colorado Plateau for the Rio Grande River drainage and the mesas of Arizona that the 19 Puebloan tribes, Zuni, and Hopi occupy to this day. It was like Chaco had been a curse, and now it was time for the Anasazi to return to their former, simple, traditional way of life.

Final Thoughts

While researching this book, and during the early phases of writing, I basked in the glow of a romanticized vision of the Chaco phenomenon. I envisioned it as Rome at its peak, a spectacular place where a vibrant culture flowered and people flourished. A place where the Anasazi had realized the society of their dreams, with great leaps in the sciences, a rich cultural tapestry of advanced organization and political institutions, a renaissance time. This was not a short-lived phenomenon; 12 generations lived and died there, the entire period lasting about as long as the United States has existed.

But that glow slowly faded as a more sobering reality began to reveal itself. These Anasazi had been a peaceful people, existing for millennia in a difficult and unpredictable terrain. And not just existing, they maximized their available resources with astounding creativity. The spectacular pottery, tools, and artifacts left behind attest to this.

Something happened in Chaco. It cannot be denied that massive feats of engineering, logistics, architecture, and organization took place, guided by injections of new knowledge and thinking not previously expressed. But something else also happened, and for this, a price was paid.

An established way of life was sucked into a societal tornado, turbulent changes tearing at the fabric of traditions honed over ages. After 12 generations, the storm subsided, and they meticulously sealed this experiment into the architecture that represented it. Then, they migrated, as they had so many times before. But this time was different. They returned to old lands to discover new problems, and within 150 years, they descended off the Colorado Plateau, settling into their current locations along the Rio Grande and the mesas of Arizona.

Even with this last migration, the remnants of a curse that began in Chaco seemed to linger. In the 16th century, the Spanish lust for gold led to a brutal oppression of the Puebloan people. In the 18th century, the westward expansion of the young United States rumbled over them like an unstoppable freight train.

Observed over a longer timeline than European Americans are accustomed, perhaps the Puebloans today understand the Chaco phenomenon lasted about as long as America has currently existed? Is this current American era viewed as another Chaco? One cannot help but see parallels.

Afterward, Comments, and Miscellany

As I reflect back on my dream that started this adventure, with the spiraling black bird following a corkscrew path into a deep sandstone canyon, the journey feels in-progress, but not yet complete. The black bird is my totem, the raven. And the shape of the spiral, I've come to learn, is very common throughout millennia of Anasazi petroglyphs. The spiraling shape is representative of multiple things, including migration. And while migration is normally associated with changes in geography, my personal migration has been one of renewed spirit, through reconnection with the wild and natural.

Petroglyphs: the Anasazi had no known written language. It is likely we will never know exactly the intent or purpose of the petroglyphs.

My Cousin Vinnie thinks I'm locked in a perpetual mid-life crisis, and she's probably right. And yes, I really do have a cousin named Vinnie. During these travels, I've been lost, (or as I prefer to say "temporarily disoriented") startled by an unseen cow running through the brush, have run out of water, and come back to the car so hungry that Pringles BBQ potato chips tasted like bacon wrapped filet. But I've enjoyed every step.

On my first trip into Grand Gulch, it started raining at four o'clock in the morning, a situation best described as "not ideal" when at the bottom of a canyon. I've seen black bear tracks, mountain lion tracks, but never come across a rattlesnake.

On my 53rd birthday, a solo trip into Coyote Gulch had two extra days added to it when it wouldn't stop raining and the creek became impassable. To add to the experience, ravens stole and ate my birthday dinner!

On a June trip to the Bannister Ruin site in Grand Gulch, I dutifully stopped at the Kane Gulch Ranger Station, watched the required video, and signed the forms. To paraphrase what I was signing: "I certify that I am not that bright, understand no one is coming to get my dumb ass if something goes wrong, and oh, if I happen to survive, I agree to carry out my own poop."

I inquired about the status of Bannister Spring, and was assured it had water. To enter this section of Grand Gulch, I had to drive to the Collins Spring trailhead, accessed via a bumpy dirt road off the highway toward

Natural Bridges National Monument. Finally there, I had to decide whether to car camp at the trailhead and get an early morning start, or head off down the trail. Feeling frisky, I loaded up and headed out. Grand Gulch was very dry, with only an occasional pothole of stagnant water. I was startled by something moving across the bedrock in front of me. Freezing in place, a frog jumped from rock to rock. A frog? Looking around, I spotted a boulder with a dark area underneath it, and wandered over to investigate. You could smell the water hidden in a dark recess under the boulder, a frog grotto if you will.

A bit further up along the trail, I came to a pothole with perhaps a half-gallon of water. I normally carry a LifeStraw with me, which is simply a fat drinking straw with a filter built into it. It is very useful when finding sources of water like this, no need to take the pack off, assemble the water filter, and repack. I lay down, beginning to use the LifeStraw to drink. As my eyes focused, I could see dozens of small tadpoles swimming around in a panic. I sipped, but left a good balance of the water for the tadpoles.

When I finally arrived at Bannister Ruin and Spring, just before dark, I found the ruin to be quite uninspiring, and the "spring" to be a thin layer of wet mud. I pitched the tent, whipped up a quick dinner, and slept underneath a sheer sandstone cliff that created a border for a spectacular display of stars.

Morning greeted me with a brilliant sunrise that quickly started heating the sandstone. I began exploring for water. If I couldn't find any, I'd need to head back before the water I carried ran out. By late morning, no reliable source was found, and I reluctantly packed up and started back, challenged by the heat of the hottest part of the day. Exhausted when I finally returned to the car after the hot, arduous climb up and out of Collins Spring Canyon, I turned the video camera on, looked into it, and simply said, "I need to find a more age-appropriate hobby."

Tip of the hat to Dave Hack for introducing me to "platypus packs", which allow for the convenient transport of a bottle of wine in a backpack. No reason we can't be civilized about this.

I'm often asked if I've had any spiritual or religious type experiences on these trips, to which I answer "maybe". The raven as totem event was entertaining, if nothing else. A later experience in Chaco may have been, or possibly it was just low blood sugar. I hiked out to the supernova petroglyph panel on a very warm day. I'd been camping and hiking by myself for about 5 days at that point, had turned off the cell phone, and wasn't interacting with anyone, save the occasional hello. On the way back, I stopped near the middle of the canyon, sat in solitude and sipped water. The air was quiet and still. Sitting there in that desolate wash, I began to sense something, thinking, *okay, there IS something here*. It wasn't positive, it wasn't negative, just a powerful sense of "energy" of some sort, nothing I've experienced before or since. I've tried to recapture it, to no avail.

My favorite place? For sheer beauty and capturing the imagination, Coyote Gulch, a tributary of the Escalante

River. It's like a smaller, private Zion, with one Anasazi site. For viewing the spectacle of Anasazi cliff dwellings without the Mesa Verde crowds, backpack to Junction Ruin, where Grand Gulch and Kane Gulch meet. Best day hike? South Mule Canyon, right off the highway near Blanding, Utah, a short, easy mile hike to the "House of Fire" ruin. Try to get there before about 9:30 in the morning and watch as the sun hits the ruin after it rises above the canyon wall. Bring your camera.

House of Fire Ruin: an easy hike near the highway west of Blanding, Utah. Early morning sun over the canyon lip lights up the red, streaky sandstone, giving the appearance the ruin is on fire.

And of course, visit Chaco Canyon. You will leave amazed.

"Of all the featherless beasts, only man, chained by his self-imposed slavery to the clock, denies the elemental fire and proceeds as best he can about his business, suffering quietly, martyr to his madness. Much to learn."
~Edward Abbey, Desert Solitaire~

Works Cited

- "The Anasazi Road System". *Archaeology News Network*, 2015, Ed. Ioannis Georgopolis. Web 19 April 2016.
- Aton, James M. and McPherson, Robert S., "River Flowing from the Sunrise: An Environmental History of the Lower San Juan". Utah State University Press: Logan. 2000. digitalcommons.usu.edu, 3 April 2016.
- Bannister, Bryant. "Tree Ring Dating of the Archeological Sites in the Chaco Canyon Region, New Mexico". *Southwest Parks and Monuments Association*: Globe, AZ, 1973. npshistory.com, N.D. Web 2 April 2016.
- Benson, Larry et al.. "Ancient Maize from Chacoan Great Houses: Where Was It Grown?". *Proceedings of the National Academy of Sciences of the United States of America* 100.22 (2003): 13111–13115. Web 2, May 2016.
- Benson, Larry V. "Who Provided Maize to Chaco Canyon After the Mid-12th Century Drought? US Geological Survey". *Journal of Archaeological Science*: Elsevier, 2010. Web 8 April 2016.
- Brown, Donald N.. "Ethnomusicology and the Prehistoric Southwest". *Ethnomusicology* 15.3 (1971): 363–378. Web 2 May 2016.
- Brown, Gary. "Some Notes on Chacoan Masonry Styles at West Ruin Aztec Ruins National Monument". *chacoarchive.org*, N.D. Web 1 April 2016.
- *Bullfrog Films*. "The Mystery of Chaco Canyon" (film). Bullfrog Films: PA, 2003.
- Bustard, Wendy. "Pueblo Bonito: When a House is Not a Home". *Pueblo Bonito: Center of the Chacoan World*. Ed. Jill Neitzel. Smithsonian Institution: Washington, 2003. (80-93)
- Cameron, Catherine M., and H. Wolcott Toll. "Deciphering the Organization of Production in Chaco Canyon". *American Antiquity* 66.1 (2001): 5–13. Web 22 April 2016.
- *Chaco Culture*. NPS: National Historical Park Guide. U.S. Dept. of the Interior, 2016.

Kyle Widner

- *Chaco Culture: Master Plan*. National Park Service Online Books, 2010. Web 3 Apr. 2016.
- Colton, Harold S.. "Sunset Crater: The Effect of a Volcanic Eruption on an Ancient Pueblo People". *Geographical Review* 22.4 (1932): 582–590. Web 2 May 2016.
- Cooper, Laurel M. "Comparative Analysis of the Chacoan Great Houses." *Arizona Archaeological and Historical Society*. Space Syntax International Symposium Proceedings II: London, 1997.
- Cornucopia, G.B..*Chaco Park Ranger Tour Guide*. Farmington CVB Tour Presentation Series, 2011.youtube 8 April 2016.
- Crown, Patricia L., and W. H. Wills. "Modifying Pottery and Kivas at Chaco: Pentimento, Restoration, or Renewal?". *American Antiquity* 68.3 (2003): 511–532. Web 1 May 2016.
- Crown, Patricia, and W. Jeffery Hurst. "Evidence of Cacao Use in Prehispanic American Southwest". *PNAS*, 2009. Web 2 April 2016.
- Crown, Patricia. *The Pueblo Bonito Mounds of Chaco Canyon: Material Culture and Fauna*. Ed. Patricia Crown. University of New Mexico: Albuquerque, 2016.
- Doxtater, Dennis. "The Great North Road as an Anasazi Origin Ritual: Chaco and Totah in Context with Triadic Plateau Structures". *University of Arizona*, N.D. Web 18 April 2016.
- Drake BL et al. "Strontium Isotopes and the Reconstruction of the Chaco Regional System: Evaluating Uncertainty with Bayesian Mixing Models*." PLoS ONE*, 2014. Web 8 April 2016.
- Drexler, Carl G. "Systemic Nesting Among the Anasazi: AD 900-1140." Nebraska Anthropologist, 2004. Web 2 May 2015.
- Earle, Timothy. "Economic Support of Chaco Canyon Society". *American Antiquity* 66.1 (2001): 26–35. Web 22 April 2016.
- English, Nathan B. et al. "Strontium Isotopes Reveal Distant Sources of Architectural Timber in Chaco Canyon, New Mexico." *Proceedings of the National Academy of Sciences of the United States of America* 98.21 (2001): 11891–11896. *PMC*. Web. 23 Apr. 2016.
- Fagan, Brian. *Chaco Canyon: Archaeologists Explore the Lives of an Ancient Society*. Oxford University Press: Oxford, 2005.

- Fewkes, J. Walter. "Hopi Snake Washing". *American Anthropologist* 11.10 (1898): 313–318.Web 1 May 2016.
- Fewkes, J. Walter. "The Butterfly in Hopi Myth and Ritual". *American Anthropologist* 12.4 (1910): 576–594. Web 2 May 2016.
- Fisher, Richard. *The Last Great Mysteries of the Chaco Canyon Anasazi Full Circle – Paquiméto Chaco and Return.* Sunracer Publications: New Mexico, 2005. Web 26 April 2016.
- Frazier, Kendrick. *People of Chaco: A Canyon and Its Culture.* W.W. Norton & Company: New York, 1999.
- Gabriel, Kathryn. "Marietta Wetherill: Life with the Navajos in Chaco Canyon." *University of New Mexico Press*: Albuquerque, 1992.
- Hall, Stephen A. "Prehistoric Vegetation and Environment at Chaco Canyon". *American Antiquity* 53.3 (1988): 582–592. Web 22 April 2016.
- Hamilton, James. "Threatening Rock". *NPS Region III Quarterly Report*, 1939.npshistory 12 April 2016.
- Hanna, Lisa, and David Hanna. *Chaco Culture National Historic Park Exotic Flora Species.* Prescott College: Prescott, 2004.
- Floyd, Hanna. Hanna 2004 Exotic Flora Species, 3 April 2016.
- Heitman, Carrie, "Houses Great and Small: Reevaluating the 'House' in Chaco Canyon, New Mexico". *Anthropology Faculty Publications University of Nebraska*, 2007. Web 8 April 2016.
- Judd, Neil M.."The Architectural Evolution of Pueblo Bonito". *Proceedings of the National Academy of Sciences of the United States of America* 13.7 (1927): 561–563. Web 26 April 2016.
- Judd, Neil M. "Everyday Life in Pueblo Bonito: As Disclosed by the National Geographic Society's Archeologic Explorations in Chaco Canyon National Monument, New Mexico". *National Geographic Magazine*: Washington, 1925.
- Judd, Neil M. "The Material Culture of Pueblo Bonito". *Smithsonian Institute*, 1954. Forgotten Books (print), 2015.
- Judd, Neil M. "The Use of Adobe in Prehistoric Dwellings of the Southwest. *United States National Museum*, 1916. Harvard University, 2008. Web 6 April 2016.

Kyle Widner

- Kantner, John. "Ancient Roads, Modern Mapping: Evaluating Chaco Anasazi Roadways Using GIS Technology. Expedition 39.3, 1997.
- Kantner, John. "Chaco Roads". *Evaluating Models of Chaco: A Virtual Conference*. Ed. Stephen Lekson. University of Colorado, 1997. Web 16 April 2016.
- Koenig, Seymour H. "Stars, Crescents, and Supernovae in Southwestern Indian Art". *Journal for the History of Astronomy, Archaeoastronomy Supplement*, Vol. 10, p.S39, 1979. Web 26 April 2016.
- Kohler, Timothy A., and Kathryn Kramer. "Raiding for Women in the Pre-Hispanic Northern Pueblo Southwest? A Pilot Examination." *Department of Anthropology Washington State University*: Pullman, 2006.
- Krupp, E.C. "Echoes of the Ancient Skies: The Astronomy of Lost Civilizations". *Oxford University Press*, 1994.
- Lekson, Stephen. "A History of the Ancient Southwest". *Lecture*: Verde Valley Archaeological Center, 05 May 2011. Web 7 Apr. 2016.
- Lekson, Stephen H.. *"Review of Relation of 'Bonito' Paleo-Channels and Base-Level Variations to Anasazi Occupation, Chaco Canyon, New Mexico"*. *Journal of Anthropological Research* 59.3 (2003): 360–361. Web 2 May 2016.
- Lekson, Stephen H."Chaco Death Squads: Two New Books Address Prehistoric Warfare in the Southwest; One Suggests a Reign of Terror by a Warrior Cult from Mexico". *Archaeology* 52.3 (1999): 67–73. Web 1 April 2016.
- Lekson, Stephen. "Chaco Matters". *The Archaeology of Chaco Canyon: An Eleventh Century Pueblo Regional Center*. Ed. Stephen Lekson. School of American Research Press: Santa Fe, 2006.
- Lekson, Stephen. *The Chaco Meridian: One Thousand Years of Political Power in the Ancient Southwest*. Rowman & Littlefield: Lanham, 2015.
- Lister, Robert and Florence Lister. *Chaco Canyon: Archaeology and Archaeologists*. University of New Mexico Press: Albuquerque, 1981.

- Loftin, John D. "Supplication and Participation: The Distance and Relation of the Sacred in Hopi Prayer Rites". *Anthropos* 81.1/3 (1986): 177–201. Web 29 April 2016.
- Marshall, Anne Lawrason. "The Siting of Pueblo Bonito." *Pueblo Bonito: Center of the Chacoan World.* Ed. Jill Neitzel. Smithsonian Institution: Washington, 2003.
- Mathien, Frances Joan. "The Organization of Turquoise Production and Consumption by the Prehistoric Chacoans". *American Antiquity* 66.1 (2001): 103–118. Web 2 May 2016.
- Mattson, Hannah. "Gray Ware from the Pueblo Bonito Mounds." *The Pueblo Bonito Mounds of Chaco Canyon: Material Culture and Fauna.* Ed. Patricia Crown. University of New Mexico Press: Albuquerque, 2016.
- McClatchy, Leo, Ed. "Threatening Rock Crashes". *NPS Region III Quarterly Report*, 1941. NPS History, 12 April 2016.
- McNitt, Frank. "Richard Wetherill: Anasazi Pioneer Explorer of Southwestern Ruins". *University of New Mexico Press*: Albuquerque, 1966.
- Metcalf, Mary P. "Construction Labor at Pueblo Bonito." *Pueblo Bonito: Center of the Chacoan World.* Ed. Jill Neitzel. Smithsonian Institution: Washington, 2003. (72-79).
- *National Park Service.* "Comparative Chronology: Pecos Classification - Chaco Classification".nps.gov, 2016. 1 April 2016.
- Neitzel, Jill E. "Artifact Distribution at Pueblo Bonito". *Pueblo Bonito: Center of the Chacoan World.* Ed.
- Jill Neitzel. Smithsonian Institution: Washington, 2003.
- Neitzel, Jill E. "Three Questions about Pueblo Bonito". *Pueblo Bonito: Center of the Chacoan World.* Ed. Jill Neitzel. Smithsonian Institution: Washington, 2003.
- Palmer, Phyllis. "Burial Customs in Small House Sites in Chaco Canyon", 1941. *chacoarchive.org*, 1 May 2016.
- Parsons, Elsie Clews. "Some Aztec and Pueblo Parallels". *American Anthropologist* 35.4 (1933): 611–631. Web 2 May 2016.
- Pepper, George."Pueblo Bonito". *The United States Natural History Museum*, 1920.

Kyle Widner

- Peregrine, Peter N. "Matrilocality, Corporate Strategy, and the Organization of Production in the Chacoan World". *American Antiquity* 66.1 (2001): 36–46. Web 2 May 2016.
- Plog, Stephen, and Adam S. Watson. "The Chaco Pilgrimage Model: Evaluating the Evidence from Pueblo Alto". Web 25 April 2016.
- Plog, Stephen, and Carrie Heitman. "Hierarchy and Social Inequality in the American Southwest, A.D. 800–1200". *PNAS*, 107:46, 16 Nov. 2010. Web 10 Apr. 2016
- Plog, Stephen. "Ritual and Cosmology in the Chaco Era". *Religious Transformation in the Late Pre-Hispanic Pueblo World*. Eds. Glowacki, Donna, and Scott VanKeuren. University of Arizona Press: Phoenix, 2011. (50-65).
- Plog, Stephen. "Exploring the Ubiquitous Through the Unusual: Color Symbolism in Pueblo Black-on-white Pottery". *American Antiquity* 68.4 (2003): 665–695. Web 1 May 2016.
- Potter, James. "Pots, Parties, and Politics: Communal Feasting in the American Southwest". *American Antiquity* 65.3 (2000): 471–492. Web 25 April 2016.
- Potter, James. "Power and Negotiation through Material Culture: The Case of the Chaco Regional System". *Kroeber Anthropological Society Papers*: Berkeley, 1992. Web 21 April 2016.
- *Reading Eagle*. "Not a Calendar: Scientists Dispute Theory, Says Sun Dagger in New Mexico is Probably an Ancient Shrine." Reading Eagle, 1984. Web 26 April 2016.
- Reed, Paul. "Chaco's Northern Prodigies: Salmon, Aztec, and the Ascendancy of the Middle San Juan Region after AD 1100". *University of Utah Press*: Salt Lake City, 2008.
- Reed, Paul, F. *The Puebloan Society of Chaco*. Greenwood Press: Westport, 2004.
- Reyman, Jonathan E. "On Spiral Motifs at Fajada Butte: Perpetuating Misinformation". *Current Anthropology* 27.2 (1986): 155–155. Web 26 April 2016.
- Ruskamp, John Jr. "The Hooper Ranch Pueblo Sun Dagger Shrine Revisited-Revealing Greater Regional Significance.Academia.edu, 2013. Web 26 April 2016.

Kyle Widner

- Saitta, Dean J. "Power, Labor, and the Dynamics of Change in Chacoan Political Economy". *American Antiquity* 62.1 (1997): 7–26. Web 24 April 2016.
- Sebastian, Lynne. "The Chaco Anasazi: Sociopolitical Evolution in the Prehistoric Southwest. *"Cambridge University Press*: Melbourne, 1992.
- Sofaer, Anna, and Rolf M. Sinclair. "On 'Perpetuating Misinformation': A Reply to Reyman". *Current Anthropology* 27.4 (1986): 372–372. Web 26 April 2016.
- Sofaer, Anna, and The Solstice Project. "Chaco Astronomy: An Ancient American Cosmology." *Ocean Tree Books*: Santa Fe, NM. 2008.
- Sofaer, Anna, and The Solstice Project. *The Mystery of Chaco Canyon: A Film Study Guide.* Bullfrogfilms.com, 2003. 5 April 2016.
- Sofaer, Anna, et al. "The Great North Road: A Cosmographic Expression of the Chaco Culture of New Mexico". The Solstice Project Research Papers. *World Archaeoastronomy*, edited by A. F. Aveni, New York: Cambridge University Press, 1989. Web 16 April 2016.
- Stuart, David and Susan Moczygemba-McKinsey. *Anasazi America: Seventeen Centuries on the Road from Center Place.* David Stuart: Albuquerque, 2000.
- Titiev, Mischa. "Two Hopi Myths and Rites". *The Journal of American Folklore* 61.239 (1948): 31–43. Web 29 April 2016.
- Toll, H. Wolcott. "Making and Breaking Pots in the Chaco World". *American Antiquity* 66.1 (2001): 56–78. Web 30 April 2016.
- VanDyke, Ruth. "The Chaco Connection: Bonito Style Architecture in Outlier Communities." Ruth Van Dyke: University of Arizona, 1998. Web 21 April 2016.
- Van Dyke, Ruth M. "Great Kivas in Time Space and Society." *The Architecture of Chaco Canyon, New Mexico*. Ed. Lekson, Stephen. University of Utah Press: Salt Lake City, 2007. (93-126).
- Van Dyke, Ruth M. "Memory, Meaning, and Masonry: The Late Bonito Chacoan Landscape". *American Antiquity* 69.3 (2004): 413–431. Web 30 April 2016.

214

Kyle Widner

- Vivian, Gordon, and Tom Mathews. "Kin Kletso: A Pueblo III Community in Chaco Canyon, New Mexico". *Southwest Parks and Monuments Association*: Globe, AZ, 1973. pshistory.com, 1967. Web 2 April 2016.
- Vivian, R. Gwinn et al. "Chaco Economy and Ecology."*The Archaeology of Chaco Canyon: An Eleventh Century Pueblo Regional Center.* Ed. Stephen Lekson. School of American Research Press: Santa Fe, 2006.
- Vivian, R. Gwinn, and Bruce Hilpert. "The Chaco Handbook: An Encyclopedic Guide", 2nd Ed. *The University of Utah Press*: Salt Lake City, 2012.
- Vivian, R. Gwinn. "The Chacoan Prehistory of the San Juan Basin". *Academic Press*: New York, 1990.
- Vivian, R. Gwinn. "Living in Chaco: Interpreting Chaco" (*speech*). *Tea and Archaeology Presentation*, 2012youtube, 8 April 2016.
- Vivian, R. Gwinn. "Kluckhohn Reappraised: The Chacoan System as an Egalitarian Enterprise". *Journal of Anthropological Research* 45.1 (1989): 101–113. Web 22April 2016.
- Washburn, Dorothy K. "Pattern Symmetries of the Chaco Phenomenon" .*American Antiquity* 76.2 (2011): 252–284. Web 28 April 2016.
- Watson, Adam S. et al. "Early Procurement of Scarlet Macaws and the Emergence of Social Complexity in Chaco Canyon, NM." *Proceedings of the National Academy of Sciences of the United States of America* 112.27 (2015): 8238–8243. *PMC*. Web. 2 Apr. 2016.
- Watson, Adam. "Long-distance Wood Procurement and the Chaco Florescence". PNAS, 113(5), 2015.
- Wicklein, John. "Spirit Paths of the Anasazi". *Archaeology* 47.1 (1994): 36–41. Web 22 April 2016.
- Wills, W. H., et al. "Prehistoric Deforestation at Chaco Canyon?" *Proceedings of the National Academy of Sciences of the United States of America* 111.32 (2014): 11584–11591. *PMC*. Web. 2 Apr. 2016.
- Wills, W. H.. "On the Trail of the Lonesome Pine: Archaeological Paradigms and the Chaco 'Tree of Life'". *American Antiquity* 77.3 (2012): 478–497. Web 24 April 2016.

Kyle Widner

- Windes, Thomas C., and Dabney Ford. "The Chaco Wood Project: The Chronometric Reappraisal of Pueblo Bonito". *American Antiquity* 61.2 (1996): 295–310. Web 22 April 2016.
- Windes, Thomas. "This Old House: Construction and Abandonment at Pueblo Bonito." *Pueblo Bonito: Center of the Chacoan World,* Jill Neitzel. ED. Smithsonian Institution: Washington, 2003. (15-32)
- Zeilik, Michael. "A Reassessment of the Fajada Butte Solar Marker". *Journal for the History of Astronomy, Archaeoastronomy Supplement*, 1985.

Kyle Widner

About Kyle Widner

Kyle Widner has a diverse business and personal background, from professional baseball prospect, to US Air Force officer, to internet entrepreneur. He has built and sold two internet based businesses; an e-commerce network to the RAF private equity group in 2008, and a biofeedback software company to Unyte Health of Canada in 2016. He is currently developing historical and educational 3D computer simulations of Chaco Canyon and other areas. Learn more at Shadowplay.com.

Kyle holds an MBA from Thunderbird, the American Graduate School of International Management.

He currently resides in Boulder City, Nevada, with his wife Jean, two cats, and two dogs. An avid hiker and backpacker, he makes several trips per year to the Four Corners region.

Made in the USA
Middletown, DE
18 February 2018